Camden Lock and the Market

OPEN
AS USUAL!

CANT

F
FRANCES LINCOLN LIMITED
PUBLISHERS

Camden Lock
and the Market

Caitlin Davies
Special Photography **Nigel Ramdial**

Dedication

To Lock traders past, present and future,
and in memory of Helen Scott Lidgett

Frances Lincoln Limited
www.franceslincoln.com

Camden Lock and the Market
Copyright © Frances Lincoln Limited 2013
Text copyright © Caitlin Davies 2013
All photographs © Nigel Ramdial 2013
Except where otherwise specified on page 175
Map © David Fathers, joemoon.co.uk
First Frances Lincoln edition 2013

A catalogue record for this book is available
from the British Library.

978-0-7112-3381-2

Printed and bound in China

1 2 3 4 5 6 7 8 9

Page 1 A neon sign entices shoppers into Camden Lock
Pages 2–3 The iconic Camden Lock bridge sign, painted by
John Bulley in the 1980s
Right A punk takes a rest on Chalk Farm Bridge

Contents

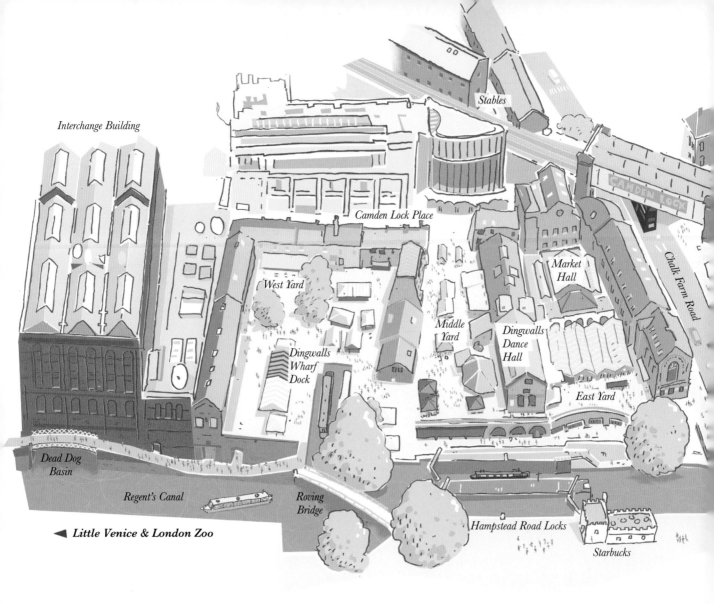

Interchange Building

Stables

Camden Lock Place

West Yard

Market Hall

Dingwalls Wharf Dock

Middle Yard

Dingwalls Dance Hall

East Yard

Chalk Farm Road

Dead Dog Basin

Regent's Canal

Roving Bridge

Hampstead Road Locks

Starbucks

◄ **Little Venice & London Zoo**

Map

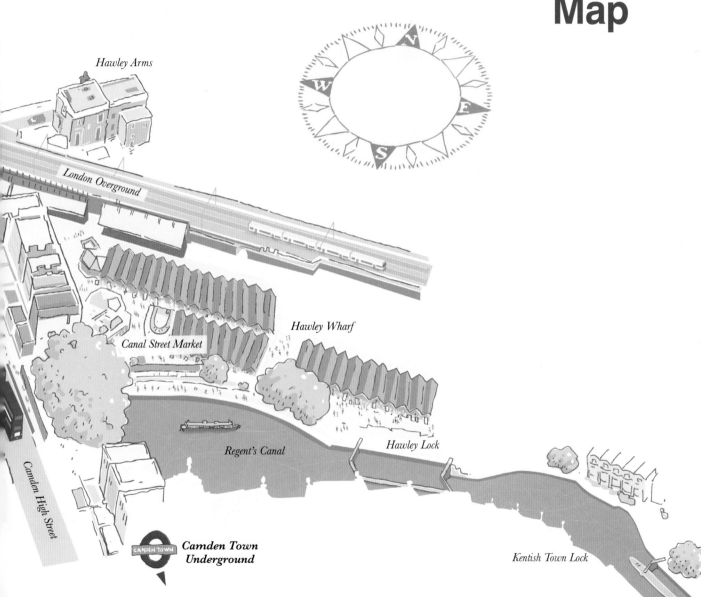

Hawley Arms

London Overground

Canal Street Market

Hawley Wharf

Camden High Street

Regent's Canal

Hawley Lock

Kentish Town Lock

Camden Town Underground

Prologue
The Story of Camden Lock

It's nine o'clock on a grey December morning and Camden High Street is virtually empty. A punk with a purple Mohican walks by, hand in hand with her mother. They stop outside a shop selling 'I love London' t-shirts and then stroll across a hump-backed bridge, pausing to look down over the Regent's Canal, one of London's best-known waterways, where in summer months pleasure boats grind and slosh through water the colour of rippling iron. The punk and her mother walk on, heading towards a turquoise painted railway bridge where giant yellow lettering announces their destination: Camden Lock, home to the world-famous market.

Every year five million visitors flock to this site to buy clothes and food, to hunt for antiques and jewellery, to listen to music. Yet strictly speaking there is no Camden Lock; it's the most famous lock in the world that doesn't exist.

Instead there are three dual locks in the area, built in the early 1800s as part of the Regent's Canal. To the left of the humpbacked bridge is Hampstead Road Lock, once the site of an ambitious new water-saving design, while to the right are Hawley and Kentish Town locks. Together they formed what one Victorian visitor described as 'a sort of water staircase of gigantic dimensions'.

The towpath where horses once pulled narrowboats is overhung with weeping willows; in the distance the old lockkeeper's cottage is now a branch of Starbucks. A sign gives directions: six miles to the Thames at Limehouse, 302 miles to Liverpool. A roving bridge links the two banks of the canal, where on the other side a group of school children run shrieking along. They pass the back of the Interchange warehouse, an ancient hub for transferring goods, and then cross over Dead Dog Basin, where canal boats once sheltered in an underground wharf.

Left Hampstead Road Lock is a set of dual locks, built in the early 1800s
Above A wintery scene on the Regent's Canal. The locks near Camden Market once formed 'a water staircase of gigantic dimensions'

At the entrance to Camden Lock's East Yard men are busy unloading a van laden with vegetables and other supplies for the food sellers. A giant festive stocking hangs from the wall of the grand Market Hall building, a neon sign advertises 'stalls this way'. 'Get all your Christmas presents here!' calls a man selling laminated blocks with names like 'nirvana', 'nostalgia', and 'way of righteousness'. Is he selling well? 'The English are not that visually open,' he says with a shrug. 'Italians are the best, I've sold to a few of them already this morning.'

The air inside the Market Hall is bright, footsteps echo on the patterned tiled floor. Seven rows of stalls, bordered by small shops, sell knitwear, jewellery, bottles turned into clocks, toys, painted boxes, prints of London scenes and Banksy murals. Many stalls assure customers that the items are handmade – from soaps to bags and hats. A sign above a collection of finger puppets warns 'no photos', but this doesn't deter an American woman with a large camera; in fact everyone seems to be a tourist, and everyone seems to have a camera.

Delicate blue and white fairy lights sway between the stalls, a tinselled miniature Christmas tree stands at the entrance to a shop, angels hang from a doorway. Above is the high airy roof, which resembles an old railway station. The air is full of the murmur of voices, like passengers politely awaiting the arrival of a train, a mix of accents and languages from all over the world.

Upstairs are more stalls selling tea, pashminas, baby bibs and leather purses. A Spanish girl complains she's cold as she waits for her mother to try on a scarf, a Japanese couple inspects a showcase of rings, three young French men sniff hand cream. There's a bang of a door and a rattle of keys as a man opens up his shop for the day. A trader bites into a bacon sandwich, his breath a stream of white in the frosty air. A stallholder fiddles with her hair and reads a newspaper while she still has the chance; Christmas is coming; in a few hours the place will be packed.

Forty years ago this Market Hall was just a small outside space, with a handful of stalls set on a dirty cobbled yard. I worked here as a teenager with my friend Gina, paid 50p an hour to sell handmade badges in the shape of chocolate bars and crisp packets that we'd shrunk in the oven and attached to safety pins. We worked for a Russian man, how we met him I can't remember, but it was exciting being on a stall, the ideal place from which to watch people. Our neighbours sold clothes, long white granddad shirts and army surplus trousers. One day Freddy Mercury came by, and everyone stopped to watch this glamorous pop star being swallowed up in the crowds.

Christmas was always my favourite time of year; the wooden stalls were brightly lit, the air sweet with the smell of mulled wine. Conditions are luxurious compared to then, no tarpaulin sheets heavy with rainwater, no need for charcoal hand warmers, no desperate search for a nearby toilet.

In the past forty years the original market has expanded beyond belief, across the various yards, into renovated warehouses and new buildings. Other markets have sprung up under different ownership, the next-door Stables Market, Canal Street Market on the other side of Chalk Farm Road, and Buck Street Market further down Camden High Street. Together with the council-run Inverness Street Market, they form the largest street market in the UK. But it all started here, in the East Yard.

Camden Lock began life as a collection of craft workshops, followed by a market. But this would only be temporary; a motorway would soon come cutting through north London, the market wouldn't last long. But it did.

In the early 1970s, Camden High Street was empty on a Sunday. These were the days before legalised Sunday trading or Sunday drinking, and when north London only had a handful of weekend markets. Today the High Street is so crowded on a Sunday you can barely breathe, and between 1pm and 5pm Camden Town tube station, built on the site of a former workhouse, is exit only. The market is open every day of the week, from around 11am to 6pm. And the only day it's closed is Christmas Day.

An archway leads from the Market Hall to the Middle Yard, where the cobbles are wet and the air smells of coffee. To the left, on the edge of the yard, is Dingwalls Dance Hall, one of Camden's first music venues, which has been hosting live gigs since 1973, with world-renowned bands, such as Frank Zappa, Bo Diddley, the Clash and the Stranglers.

Ahead is the West Yard where a shaft of lemon-yellow winter sunlight illuminates the trees and a man in overalls mops the top of a traditional narrowboat. This is the food area, a United Nations of offerings: pie and mash, jerk chicken, Ethiopian cuisine, Spanish tapas, kangaroo burgers. Pan lids clatter, a radio plays an old Beatles tune, a stallholder pulls a suitcase rattling across the yard, pigeons swoop down and are gone. Forty years ago there was only one food stall in the market and until very recently none in the West Yard at all.

Behind the food area is a row of shops, selling gift cards, carpets, books and boots. These were the original crafts units; where local artisans, some of whom have gone on to establish international reputations, sold their wares out of converted horse stables. To the right, in Camden Lock Place, where there are more London t-shirts on sale, a stallholder has written the price of his CDs with black pen on a banana.

Many locals decry the current state of the place, the crowds, the noise and the litter, the type of goods on offer, the way small independent shops have been pushed out of the High Street to make way for chain stores. But there's no doubt the market has become globally renowned, especially for fashion. Famed for its hippy flares and cheesecloth smocks in the early 1970s, followed by ripped punk t-shirts, chains and bondage, the flamboyant outfits of the New Romantics in the 80s, goth corsets and platform boots, and the lycra and leggings of the 90s, it's been the birthplace of numerous clothing brands. Designers and former stallholders have gone on to open West End shops and launch multi-million pound fashion empires.

I sit in a second floor teashop, drinking a chilli and chocolate tea with Dr Bill Fulford, a neatly suited professorial-looking gentleman who works in philosophy and medicine at Warwick and Oxford universities. Along with his old school friend, chartered surveyor Peter Wheeler, they are the original market founders. In the early 1970s the two men went into partnership converting old houses into flats before looking around for a new project. 'We offered a £100 reward to anyone who found us a good site,' says Bill. 'A friend of mine who lived in Camden was walking over the roving bridge one day and he looked at this place by the water and he thought, "I wonder if Bill would be interested in this?"'

Bill was, and he and Peter applied for a lease for what was then a run-down timber yard belonging to T E Dingwalls. A council rubbish-processing plant on the other side of the canal was the liveliest thing there was, in an area generally seen as tough, deprived, damaged and empty.

But within a few years Camden Lock had become the place to see and be seen, trends started here and quickly went global, and the list of famous market visitors reads like a Who's Who from the world of music and fashion; Mick Jagger, Bob Dylan, Bette Midler, Eric Clapton, Barbra Streisand, David Bowie, Naomi Campbell, Giorgio Armani.

A teashop customer comes over and politely interrupts. 'Excuse me,' she says, 'but I couldn't help overhearing you talking about the market, my daughter lives in New York and she always said Camden is *the* place to be.' It wasn't always the case. Some 200 years

ago this area was open countryside and Camden was a small, new town. Then came the Regent's Canal; warehouses sprang up alongside its banks and business boomed. But as canal traffic declined, Camden Town became a place of overcrowding and violence. A hundred years later, in the early 1970s, the area was home to bomb-damaged buildings, the canalside warehouses were no longer in use; the locks were bordered by potholed towpaths closed to the general public. And then came the market.

The history of Camden Lock is one of dereliction and rejuvenation, of creativity versus commercialisation, of four decades of collaboration and in-fighting. The relationship between traders and management has often been fraught, and while stallholders tend to help each other out, to look after each other's stalls, to share the good days and the bad, there is always a need to protect territory and goods, and competition for pitches has often been fierce. Many traders have worked here on and off for decades, some continuing a family tradition. Some started with a Saturday job and never looked back, others made a spur of the moment decision to try their luck on a stall and ended up forging a whole new career. People have found friendships, business partners and love; relationships have been made, and broken. 'In any human activity there are tensions,' says Bill. 'In a family for example, it's what you do with those tensions that matters and how you balance the ideas. Conflict sells and it can be creative and that's what has worked at the Lock.'

Careers have started – and ended – at Camden Lock. Fortunes have been made, and sometimes lost, over night. People have learned first-hand what sells, and what doesn't. Market trading is a cash business, stallholders can be cagey about their income, and sales fluctuate wildly thanks to the great British weather. Today handmade, locally sourced craft has been largely replaced by mass-produced goods, and while backpacking students once travelled to Asia and brought back unusual items, now low-cost travel means imported 'ethnic' goods are everywhere.

Forty years ago this was an industrial dead zone. How was it transformed into a fashionable locale, and what stories can the stallholders tell in this, the market that forever changed the face of Camden Town and put this north London postcode on the world map?

Camden Lock has become the place to see and be seen, especially for those on the hunt for fashion

1. Camden Town & The Regent's Canal

Deep down under Camden Lock, ghostly navvies labour on
Horseshoes clop across the bridge and a phantom barge is floating in
From 'Canal' the Musical by Rob Inglis, 2008

Camden Town started life in 1791; a five-street town built on an estate belonging to Charles Pratt, the 1st Earl of Camden who took his title from his family home in Kent. Before this, the area had been largely farmland supplying milk to the city, its few existing roads haunted by highway robbers. Then, in the late 1700s local landlords began vying to get people to build on their land, sparking something of a speculation boom.

At first Camden Town, built east of today's High Street, was an affluent place, a spill-off from the fashionable village estates around Regent's Park. It was also popular with artists, who could walk to work in the galleries of the West End but still live relatively cheaply in the country. Then, in 1820 the Regent's Canal arrived and, aside from the railways, nothing would have a greater impact on the area until the birth of the market 150 years later.

The aim of the Regent's Canal was to link the Grand Junction Canal to the Regent's Canal Dock (later known as Limehouse Basin) and the River Thames, carrying goods from the industrial Midlands to London and transporting goods inland from the city docks. The idea for the canal came from boat owner Thomas Homer who approached noted architect John Nash, who was about to produce a comprehensive plan for his friend the Prince Regent to redevelop parts of north London. In 1812 the Company of the Proprietors of The Regent's Canal was formed, with Nash a company director and Homer the land surveyor, and work began the same year. There was considerable press coverage. 'Few public Works have of late excited greater public interest,' reported the *Morning Chronicle,* 'than the proposed Canal from Paddington, through Marybone Park [sic], to Limehouse, called the REGENT'S CANAL.'

ENTRANCE TO THE REGENT'S CANAL, LIMEHOUSE,

TO THE REGENTS CANAL COMPANY THIS PLATE IS DEDICATED.

Published Jany 26. 1825 by Jones & Co 3 Acton Place, Kingsland Road London.

Drawn by Thos H Shepherd.

Engraved by I.J.Hav

The aim of the Regent's Canal was to carry goods from the industrial Midlands to London, and transport goods inland from the city docks

But building the new waterway was far from easy; an impressive feat of engineering, it was eight and a half miles long and required twelve locks and three tunnels. It took eight years to build, with work repeatedly delayed by land disputes, fistfights, and endless money problems. It also involved the passing of several acts of Parliament, as well as causing the death of many 'navvies', the navigator men and boys who came from all over Britain and Ireland to dig out the route by hand, using spades, picks and wheelbarrows. In one instance twelve men were buried under a bank of earth as they were widening the channel near Camden Town – only eight were dug out alive. In contractors' pay books they were referred to only by a given name – Gipsy Joe, Fancy Bob, Fighting Jack – and on Sundays they were paid in alcohol, much to the horror of local missionaries. According to local lore, four separate 'Castle' pubs were built to serve the different nationalities and avoid disputes; the Windsor, Dublin, Pembroke and Edinboro, and all but the Windsor still exist today.

Further drama came for the Regent's Canal when wealthy local landowner William Agar instructed his gardeners and servants to barricade the gateway when canal workers tried to enter his estate in 1815. In addition, Homer was found to be embezzling funds and eventually fled to sea, writing an apologetic letter to his employers, 'the fact is I durst not remain in England…. How I am to make peace with God and Man I know not.' The man whose idea the canal had been was sentenced to seven years' transportation to Australia, and according to unconfirmed reports later died in New Zealand.

The next delay in construction was due to a new design of lock at Hampstead Road, next to today's market. In 1813, noted inventor Colonel William Congreve, who had invented the rockets used in the Napoleonic Wars, patented a water-saving hydro-pneumatic lock, which would allow passing boats to go in opposite directions at the same time, in theory taking just three minutes.

The directors of the Regent's Canal Company were enthusiastic; they hired a leading engineering company to erect the new lock at Hampstead Road, and built a lock-keeper's cottage to house the pump. But the trial lock

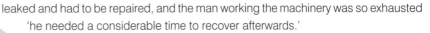

leaked and had to be repaired, and the man working the machinery was so exhausted 'he needed a considerable time to recover afterwards.'

The lock was a failure, largely because of the materials at Congreve's disposal, and in 1818 the canal company finally abandoned the idea. The equipment was auctioned for scrap, ending an expensive saga that had lasted almost seven years, and the lock had to be rebuilt.

By then the first part of the canal – from Paddington to Camden Town – had opened, on the Prince Regent's birthday on 12 August 1816. Then on 1 August 1820, the entire canal was officially launched, with the press reporting on this 'most stupendous undertaking'. Barges with bands of music made their way down the canal decorated with 'flags and streamers in profusion, boatmen wore their Sunday clothes with ribands in their hats'. The canal proprietors and other invited guests ended the trip with a 'magnificent dinner' at Limehouse, while onlookers on the towpaths fought off marauding gangs of pickpockets.

The Regent's Canal appeared to be a great success, carrying 120,000 tons of cargo in the first year, including coal, bricks, iron, lime, timber, stone, nails, glass, salt, and pottery. Two types of boats travelled the waterway, barges and narrowboats. The former had sails, lowered as the boats left the Thames. The press waxed lyrical about the picturesque barges, with *The Penny Illustrated* noting the 'robust appearance' of the bargemen due to 'the fresh breeze which they enjoy during the slow, but often pleasant, voyages from London to distant places.'

When the Regent's Canal opened in 1820 it was declared 'a most stupendous undertaking'. This picture shows workers at Hampstead Road Lock during construction of the new road bridge. The curved structure no longer exists.

But in reality conditions on the barges were harsh, and life on the cramped narrowboats was even harder. These had been in use well before the Regent's Canal, built to fit through the tunnels and locks in the Midlands, where everything was kept as narrow as possible to save money. They were popularly known as Monkey Boats, possibly after Thomas Monk who designed a boat cabin, and were owned by companies like Pickford's, Fellows, Morton & Clayton, or by individuals known as 'number ones'.

In the eighteenth century narrowboatmen had lived in cottages with their families, returning home after the working day. While they were better off than farm or factory workers, this had changed by the early nineteenth century, and when companies cut wages, families moved onto the boats rather than pay rent on a cottage. Instead of a hired crew, the boatman's wife – the 'mate' – and child – the 'boy' – did the work. Only the men got paid.

The narrowboats were pulled by horses, which walked along the towpaths, and local stabling at Camden Town could hold up to 420 horses. Injured animals were taken to a

nearby horse hospital, where the Stables Market now stands and where there still exists a network of horse tunnels.

At first, the Regent's Canal had a limited impact on Camden Town; it was merely a route to get goods through the area. But then industry developed alongside the waterway, with builders' merchants and gas works, open wharves, warehouses and yards. Battlebridge Basin, built near King's Cross in 1822, was at various times home to timber and stone yards, a steam flour mill, corn and salt warehouses, beer bottlers, stables, coal merchants and a saw mill. It was also the site of an ice house, belonging to Swiss Italian Carlo Gatti, who made a name for himself selling the popular penny ice. Ice was a much-needed commodity in the days before modern refrigeration, and while it was often taken from the Regent's Canal in the winter, the amounts were small and not always clean.

In the 1820s ice began to be imported from Norway, unloaded from ships at Limehouse and carried along the Regent's Canal to some of the biggest ice wells in London, including one near the back of today's Camden Lock Market. In 1857 Gatti bought 400 tons of Norwegian ice and stored it in ice wells at Battlebridge Basin, and one of the ice wells can still be seen in the middle of the London Canal Museum, a wide black pit into which visitors regularly throw coins as if it were a wishing well.

Despite its initial success, within twenty years the Regent's Canal was under threat from a newer form of transport, the railways. The London & Birmingham Railway, the first main line into London, opened in 1837, and stations were built at King's Cross and Euston. The owners of the Regent's Canal repeatedly came up with plans to drain the water and lay down tracks, without success.

The railways brought employment and industry to Camden Town, which had now grown to 15,000 inhabitants. Charles Dickens, who lived in Camden as a child, witnessed the impact of the railways, which he described in *Dombey & Son*: 'Everywhere were bridges that led nowhere; thoroughfares that were wholly impassable…Babel towers of chimneys…carcasses of ragged tenements, and fragments of unfinished walls and arches.'

The Camden Goods Depot was built alongside the canal in 1839, and big business moved in, including Gilbey's, the world's largest wine and spirit firm, with a distillery, storage and bottling plants in Camden. Camden High Street was soon lined with shops, its road busy with tramcars. 'The principal part (of Camden Town) has been erected within the last few years,' explained Samuel Lewis in his 1848 *Topographical Dictionary of England*; 'the houses are in general well built and regular.' There were 'elegant residences in progress of erection', and streets that were 'wide and regularly formed… lighted and partially paved.'

But when residents in King's Cross were thrown out of their homes to make way for factories, they crowded into wherever they could, most heading to the backstreets of Camden. While large expensive houses remained, they were now being broken down into flats and rooms, often with two families squeezed into one room, and where women often sought work as prostitutes and 'mangle girls'.

An 1864 music hall song summed up the popular image of Camden Town when a gentleman's future wife takes him to meet her washerwoman mother.

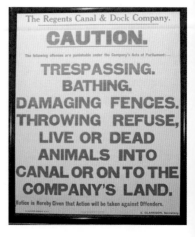

Above The Regent's Canal & Dock Company put up signs to prevent trespassing on the towpath
Right Chalk Farm Road facing north with the railway bridge in the background, in the early 1900s. On the left is where the Market Hall is today, with the Camden Lock clock still in the same position

'She was such a nice young girl,
Forget her I never shall,
She wore high heel boots and a green silk gown,
And her mother kept a mangle up at Camden Town.'

But when the couple are accosted by 'some boys on mischief bound' who cry, 'Look at Sal the mangle girl with her swell', they decide to head to Hackney instead.

By the end of the nineteenth century Camden Street was 'a good broad street', according to social researcher Charles Booth, but on Camden Road 'some quite poor people sometimes found here.' The High Street was 'an important thoroughfare with many good shops; 'bus route and trams', but nearby Little Clarendon Street was 'the worst spot in the immediate n'hood and a good many prostitutes and amateurish thieves are living here.' Locals knew it as 'Little Hell'. Further west near Chalk Farm Road, Booth found 'the first barefooted lad I have seen in the whole of the division…v low class; rowdy at night.'

Camden Town, once a place of elegant buildings and neatly paved streets, was now a sleazy underworld, with decaying dwellings and lodging houses. The High Street in Edwardian times remained busy with shops and trams, as well as music halls and theatres, but it was no longer the salubrious place it had once been and the gap between rich and poor was growing wider than ever.

In 1885 Harper's *New Monthly Magazine* reported country-like scenes around Regent's Park, with fine residences, high walls and stuccoed gentility. Then came 'the workaday world of warehouse, of saw-mills and of foundries. This is Camden New Town, its wharves piled high with timber and tiles, its workshops loud with buzzing saws and with hammers on boiler plates.'

The canal cut through a diverse social landscape, among 'poor dwellings and wealthy workshops; between the little back yards of houses and high warehouse walls; under stone bridges over which rumble vans and carts…past wharves whereon is piled everything in the world with which men are able to build'. The pungent smell of malt filled the air, gas works and foundries belched out smoke and flame, and visitors were treated to the sight of 'macaroni…hung out in endless hanks and skeins'.

The Regent's Canal was now a place of danger and tragedy. In theory the canal and its towpaths were closed to the public, particularly in Camden where there were so many valuable

Top left Britain's canals could be lethal for children, especially when they used them as summertime bathing spots
Bottom left Dingwalls Wharf at Camden Town, once part of the 'workaday world of warehouse and saw-mills'

goods – from building materials to gin. But this didn't stop people from trespassing, and cases of suicide, drowning and murder littered the pages of the local and national press. In 1868 the *Penny Illustrated* reported, 'suicides from bridges in London are unfortunately of too frequent occurrence to command much of the public attention' but it noted a case 'somewhat out of the common run of the chronicles of self destruction' when two teenage girls, 'both servants out of places' leaped into the Regent's Canal, locked in each other's arms.

The canal also became seriously polluted, driving one letter writer to object to 'the abominable smells' in warm weather: 'It is my lot daily to cross the canal…and for weeks the stench which arises from the Water has been most dreadful.' Passing barges made 'foul gases rise' and he feared for the health of children who gathered on bridges to watch the boats pass.

But many locals also used the canal as a summertime bathing spot, in the days when few people knew how to swim, and some residents were appalled by the habit of naked bathing. *The Graphic* expressed sympathy for those trying to escape 'the late unprecedented heat' in 1872, but wanted an end to the practice of those 'making themselves an intolerable nuisance to those who dwell on the banks of the Regent's Canal'. It suggested more baths be built for the 'lower classes'. Not long after, a group of twenty-five boys were each fined two shillings for offending public decency.

If the first eighty years of the Regent's Canal had helped transform Camden Town into a heavily industrialised area, carrying much-needed goods from far and wide, its fortunes in the twentieth century would be more mixed.

Camden Town in the early 1900s was a bleak place, depicted by artists like Walter Sickert as full of desperate inhabitants living in impoverished lodging houses, while the once impressive Regent's Canal was lined with shanty houses overshadowed by looming warehouses. 'It was a very dark and dirty area,' remembers Jack Whitehead, who first visited Camden in the mid-1920s as a young boy. 'All the buildings were sooty. But it did have exciting shops, like the famous animal shop in Parkway where a girl sat outside with a python.'

Camden was now known for its animal shops, and for the Regent's Park Zoo which had opened to the public in 1847, and there were some hair-raising escapes. In one instance an eight-month-old leopard bit its way out of a cage at an animal dealer's shop, and was later recaptured in a backyard. Then came the sighting of a sea lion 'disporting itself in the Regent's Park canal', according to an eye-witness who 'stoutly maintained his ability to identify a sea lion when he saw one'. The authorities set out with nets, a crate and a bucket of fish, only to discover it was an otter that had escaped from the zoo two months earlier.

The 1930s saw a brief resurgence in canal trade after the Regent's Canal Company bought the Grand Junction Canal and the Warwick Canal, merging the three as the Grand Union Canal Company. Cargo rose from 8,999 tons in 1931 to 168,638 tons in 1941 – more than in 1820 when the canal had opened. Goods also included 'a supply of sea water' taken from the Bay of Biscay all the way to Regent's Park for the zoo's aquarium.

But Camden remained an impoverished place, and it suffered extensive damage during World War Two. Just over 600 high explosive bombs fell on the borough of St Pancras, including one on Camden Town Tube Station; in total almost a thousand people were killed and around 18,000 houses damaged or demolished. In 1943 a local artist painted a hospital scene entitled 'Camden Town Kids Don't Cry' showing a 'typical London child of workaday parentage' injured after an air-raid.

Towards the end of the war, traffic again increased on the canal as an alternative to the bomb-damaged railways. David Perman remembers being taken along the Regent's Canal in 1945 as a nine-year-old, by his grandfather George Rockingham, 'He used to take me on the barges on a Saturday. He picked me up at the City Road Lock, and he talked all the way to Paddington.' His grandfather's job was to deliver goods such as sugar, carpets and sacks, which then continued north by train from Paddington. These were not pretty barges, but great steel lighters with a tiller so heavy that lightermen often ended up in the canal when the tiller shifted.

After the war the Regent's Canal was nationalised, becoming part of the British Transport Commission, and the last horse-drawn commercial traffic carrying timber or coal ended in 1956. Some trade continued into the 1960s, including six pairs of boats that did the 'cocoa run' taking beans to the Cadbury factories at Bourneville. But in the great freeze of 1962-3, narrowboats transporting coal for power stations and removing factory waste were stuck fast in ice for six weeks, by the end of which canal trade was virtually dead. Two local narrowboats were driven into the canal dock at Dingwalls Wharf, where the Market Hall now stands, and the inlet filled in.

In 1963 the British Waterways Board took over responsibility for the canal, and six years later the Regent's Canal Dock was closed to shipping. Commercial traffic had

Above A post-war landscape: a uniformed man leaps
from one opening lock gate to the other at Hampstead Road
Right Looking southeast towards Hampstead Road Lock from
the canal towpath, the bridge arches over Dead Dog Basin
where boats sheltered during World War II

pretty much vanished; lorries offering 'door to door service' carried the traffic not already lost to the railway. What, then, was the future of the canal?

In 1967 The Regent's Canal Group, formed by local civic and waterways societies, produced a report, concerned that the canal had become a 'neglected backwater'. It drew up eight design schemes, with 'Hawley Basin', on the other side of Chalk Farm Road from today's market, earmarked as a potential 'lively social centre' for workshops, studios and 'music making'. But this would be dependent on a new transport development, the upcoming London Motorway Box, part of a series of motorways that would take traffic in and out of the city and whose North Cross Route would travel via Camden Town.

Despite the decline in commercial traffic, recreational use of the canal was growing, with 120 pleasure craft and residential boats using the waterway. The first boat to be licensed by the Ministry of Transport to carry trippers was the *Jason*, launched in 1951 and owned and operated by artist John James who bought it as a floating home and studio. One journalist described making the journey from Little Venice in the summer of 1952, passing 'serious fishermen and little boys after tiddlers and a friendly drunk in a beret, singing and nursing a cabbage'. Another reported that the *Jason* carried summer sightseers up and down the Regent's Canal in 'water green as the Seine'. In 1959 a new boat was launched, British Waterways' zoo Waterbus, which ran from the zoo to Little Venice. By 1965 the company had three converted narrowboats which, according to the Regent's Canal Group, carried an impressive 95,000 passengers a year. In 1968 another passenger boat started, the *Jenny Wren* owned by Paddy Walker, a wood carver and antique dealer who, in 1952, had opened a shop on Camden High Street, alongside a handful of other dealers. 'It was a light industrial, working class area,' remembers his son Roy, who was born in the mid 50s. 'Jamestown Road was a bombed, open site and from there to the tube were food shops; a fishmonger, two butchers, two bakers, shops selling poultry and game, and sweetshops.'

Paddy decided to move into the boat business, buying a semi-derelict building opposite Hawley Wharf, initially as a workshop for cabinetmakers. 'Being on the water, we got a canoe, a dingy, then a trip boat and a restaurant boat,' says Roy. 'We were the new boys on the block. The *Jason* was very busy, but they didn't pick up or drop people at Camden, while the Waterbus went between Little Venice and the zoo, so there was no one in this area.'

Right Camden Town in the 1960s had buildings that 'hadn't seen a lick of paint since the war': the timber yard at Dingwalls Wharf
Far right Passenger boat the *Jenny Wren* was launched by local antique dealer Paddy Walker in 1968, when recreational use of the canal was growing

The *Jenny Wren* was a new, purpose-built boat, and the passengers were Londoners; 'we had lots of school trips in the days before health and safety went stupid and when teachers could take kids out for the day. Regent's Park and the zoo were pretty, and going through the locks added interest.'

On land however there was virtually nothing for sightseers to see in Camden Town in the 1960s but crumbling terraces and dirty streets. 'Considering how close it was to central London it was extraordinary how run down it was,' says Peter Wheeler, one of the founders of Camden Lock. 'There were buildings that hadn't seen a lick of paint since before the war.' Old established industries like Gilbey's had moved out, partly due to the Clean Air Act of 1956 and partly because of post-war government grants which encouraged firms to move out of the city. The area's decline continued into the 70s, small businesses closed and remaining shops lost trade. After 140 years of traffic, the locks in Camden Town were surrounded by derelict land and disused warehouses, with towpaths in bad repair.

The proposed London Motorway Box meant the locks would be turned into a motorway spur, there was even a proposal to shut the canal at Camden and culvert it all the way to the Thames, and the future of Camden was uncertain. It was then that two enterprising young men had a novel idea; why not turn the old deserted timber yard at Dingwalls Wharf into a crafts place and market?

2. Dingwalls Wharf

In 1971 two old friends, Bill Fulford and Peter Wheeler, met up for the first time since their school days. Bill was now a young medical student living in Muswell Hill, who in order to pursue his dreams of research had bought a house in Hampstead and converted it into flats, while Peter had recently qualified as a chartered surveyor, with a degree in Estate Management. Together they formed a company, Northside Developments Limited, to develop flats around Clapham Common. 'Our model was to find a large old house,' explains Bill, 'and creatively produce flats that made an asset of heritage features.' Aware

that the residential boom would burst, the two men offered a £100 reward to anyone who found them a new project. It was then that a friend came across roughly an acre of land around Dingwalls Wharf in Camden Town. 'We'd been looking around the docks,' remembers Peter, 'and we wanted a project on water, because water and property are a good mix. Then Bill's friend said, "if you're looking for water why not think about the Regent's Canal?" Camden was a slightly off piste area then, with unusual venues, cheap space, pubs with bands and theatre, and a really eclectic mix of slightly unusual businesses.'

The Dingwalls site included a group of commercial buildings, on the north side of the Regent's Canal, which formed three yards. The West Yard had a wharf, with Victorian buildings on two sides, and an entrance from Commercial Place, which was a private road and home to Gilbey's No. 2 bottle store. The freehold belonged to British Waterways, and the lease was held by T E Dingwalls Ltd, a firm of shippers and specialist packers which had been on the site since 1946. The company brought timber from the London docks via the Regent's Canal and then nailed it together into wooden cases, advertising its services with

Left and Above T E Dingwalls, a packing case company, had been at the wharf since 1946. By the early 1970s they were 'just about' in operation

a huge hoarding saying 'Dingwalls and Camden Chamber of Commerce make a Good Case for You'. In 1950 Dingwalls had employed 150 people; now they were down to just fifteen. 'Dingwalls was still in operation, just about,' remembers Peter. 'They still made packing cases but they'd been overwhelmed by the change from cases to containers. Their office was a very old-fashioned outfit, where people clocked in every morning and they used a tannoy system to call the workers.'

In 1971 the Dingwalls family decided to dispose of its assets and invited offers. 'They liked our approach,' says Bill. 'We said we don't have money but we have imagination, and we're good at working with tricky old stuff. We thought it was a fabulous area to do

workshops. We wanted a place where people worked and sold, along with a restaurant and an arts cinema. They thought that was great.' Northside won an informal tender, buying 'the rump end of a twenty-five-year lease' which had around ten years to run, for £10,000, and contracts were exchanged on 13 March 1972.

The next step was to get permission from Camden Council to change the site's industrial use. 'The council wanted to knock the whole place down,' remembers Bill, 'but a planning officer called Mary Dent saw there was heritage that could be kept. We persuaded them that mixed use would be best.' Peter, who had been interested in junk shops and markets since he was a child, wanted a craft and antique market to be part of the mix. However the council advised Northside to exclude it from the original planning application. 'We were told there would have been traffic issues,' says Bill, 'which is ironic when you remember the whole area was dead, and the perception of markets then was that they were rough places, with vagrants, hawkers and pickpockets.' To Peter, the issue of traffic was a red herring: 'what the council were really concerned about was the possibility of having to pay compensation if they had to buy the property under compulsory purchase'. There was also the fact that councils then had a virtual monopoly

Far left The *Jenny Wren* outside Dingwalls Wharf.
Left The canal dock at Dingwalls Wharf
Right Northside believed the West Yard would be 'a fabulous area to do workshops'
Below An example of traditional canalware sold by David Bamford, an early resident at the wharf

on street markets, a position which they 'coveted'. Northside promised the project would be an 'exercise in positive environmental planning', to overcome 'the stagnation of Planning Blight', and basing development on the needs of the area. However the council responded that there couldn't be any long-term plans until the future of the motorway was decided. A slip road was scheduled for the east end of the site and an elevated section of motorway would run along the northern boundary. But the motorway box plan gave Northside a creative opportunity, and under the original scheme, once the motorway arrived, the market would be beneath it.

In April 1972 the council gave Northside temporary planning permission to use the site for three years, including workshops, restaurants, a waiting area for canal boats, sculpture studios, a snack bar and administration office. Northside then set up various joint companies, aware that investors were unlikely to put up large amounts of money with such a short lease, matching investment and sharing profits in future businesses such as Dingwalls Dance Hall and Tricia's Café. Planning permission was soon extended to 1980, but when Northside applied to use part of the yards and Commercial Place as a Saturday market, this was refused.

Northside hired John Dickinson as architect, and his job was to divide the old double storey horse stables in the West Yard into small units for craftspeople such as cabinetmakers, jewellers, potters, furniture repairers, and blacksmiths. John had already worked with Peter on several projects and they shared a flat they had converted back in 1967. His brief at Camden was to 'get the place lettable. The whole site was scheduled for demolition and Camden High Street would become a link to the bottom of the M1, so we had very little time. We didn't build anything, but we created shops in the West Yard, and turned a corrugated iron hut on Commercial Place into the Lock Shop. My budget was just £5,000. We made use of Dingwalls' two cranes to remove rubbish, and hired a charismatic South African builder called Louis Friedman, who had a big team of hippies and the amazing ability to galvanise men into producing their best.'

In the Middle Yard was Tricia's Café, initially run by Geoffrey Casson, which would become Le Routier, and where Dave Stewart (who would later form the Eurythmics with Annie Lennox) was one of the original front-of-house managers. There was also a crèche and a baker who 'cooked at night so the whole place was toasty warm in the morning'. The yard's floor was covered in granite setts (flat-topped cobbles) and scruffy tarmac

and 'it was a big job to remove it, but we saw the setts underneath and thought, don't they look lovely?'

John also converted a studio for photographer Eric Swayne, who'd begun his career in the early 60s, and was known for his portraits of rock stars and models, some of which are today held in the National Portrait Gallery. 'He wanted to do videos which were very new then,' remembers John, 'and we did an asphalt floor for him because that was the smoothest floor there was. For his first shoot he managed to get a Harley Davidson bike ridden up the ramp into his studio, it dripped oil and completely ruined the floor.'

As well as hiring an architect, Northside employed Cathy Palmer as office manager. She'd been working as a secretary at IBM; in 1973 she went to Northside to cover for a friend for six weeks and ended up staying thirty-nine years. 'It was a mess,' she remembers. 'My friend left me a notebook with six messages and that was it. There was a bookkeeper who came a couple of times a week and I said I could do that. I never wanted to leave because the place was always changing. Bill would say, 'would you like to go out for lunch?' and I knew I was going to be told about a new project that he and Peter were starting. There was always something new happening at Camden.'

While Northside set about transforming the old timber wharf, a handful of people moved in to live on site. Nick and Sue Herbert, who ran a musical repair workshop, stayed with their children in a boat in the Dingwalls Dock and were 'the nearest we had to security in the early days,' explains Peter Wheeler. Another resident was David Bamford who specialised in traditionally painted canal ware, and later ran Tricia's Café with his partner. He would also become, in effect, the first market manager, collecting rent and allocating stalls. Artist Wilf Scott arrived at Hampstead Road Lock by boat in the early 70s, working in the winter as a crewmember for John and Sue Duddington who were skippers for the *Bexhill* and the *Brighton*, two narrowboats built in the 1930s and then part of a fleet operated by the Union Canal Carriers. 'We came across Dingwalls Wharf, moored where Tricia's Café was and we stayed there,' remembers Wilf. 'British Waterways complained, but Dave Bamford invited us in and offered us some demolition work. One of our first jobs was to take the heavy castings from the machine shop to Rugby for scrap. We returned to Camden and ended up hiding in Dingwalls Wharf with the pair of boats, doing odd jobs for Bamford. The people who owned our boats wanted them

back, but they were our homes so we hid on them.' Wilf eventually moved off the boat and lived in a big showground wagon where the Market Hall now is, which was then known as the front yard. 'People always thought we had loads of money in there, but the Camden criminal fraternity were OK, they would alert us if it looked like someone was going to break into one of our wagons. One night there was a bang on my wagon and this man said, 'let me in, I've got to hide here because I just murdered someone'. He was big so I let him in. I think he got captured in the end.' Wilf later met his first wife, fashion photographer Caroline Arber, when she rented his showground's wagon for a location shoot.

Together with Dud (John Duddington), Wilf built a shop, 'just breeze block and lap board',

My old Dad is tall and thin
He taught himself to knit and spin
And keeps his nose above his chin
Carrying a sign saying 'Enquire Within'

Top Left Craftsperson Paolo Lurati fashioned bracelets from bent spoons and forks
Above An illustration by artist Wilf Scott, who arrived at the wharf in the early 1970s and later exhibited his work at the ICA.
Bottom Left Dingwalls Wharf was 'an empty shell until the place started to fill up with craftspeople': a sign at the end of Commercial Place advertising the workshops

opposite the entrance to what would become Dingwalls Dance Hall. The shop sold work by Sue, who was a canal art painter, as well as Wilf's drawings and prints (he later exhibited at the ICA), model steam engines, one-arm bandits defunct after the introduction of decimal currency, and old fairground equipment including showman wagons, three-ton monsters that needed to be pulled by a truck. 'The rich from Hampstead said, "oh can you get us one?"' says Wilf, 'So they bought one and then they realized, "oh my god, my Land Rover can't pull this…"' The slot machines, meanwhile, were exported to America, via John Derham Antiques on Chalk Farm Road.

In the early days Wilf remembers Dingwalls Wharf as 'just a big yard with a long shed; it was an empty shell until the place started to fill up with craftspeople. I must thank Northside, for giving us misfits a haven of peace and decadence for a few years.'

By the summer of 1972 parts of the West Yard had been successfully converted into crafts units, let at £8 a week, and the place was ready for business. Jackie Jones, who had just left Hornsey Art College, was staying with her parents nearby: 'my mother used to walk along the towpath to Inverness Street market, I was living at home, being a broke student, and one day she said, "oh they're turning the old timber yard into crafts workshops". So I went along, contacted people at college and we jumped in at the deep end and started our own business in a 400-square-foot workshop. The units were just empty shells, there were no doors and because there was a lot of wood around we built a workbench out of three-inch mahogany, then we put the doors on. The nice thing was the sociability of it all. There wasn't so much handmade jewellery then and we got a lot of publicity, we were quite unique. We were a place where normal, local people with an average salary could buy something. However one day someone came in and wanted sixty badges in the shape of a star for Ringo Starr's wedding, and he wanted it in a hurry.'

Jackie was a member of The Five Jewellers, along with Susan Hines, Karen Lawrence, Gudde Skyrme, Belinda Patterson, Beverley Phillips and David Taylor. 'We were never really the same five, and actually there were always six of us, it's just that someone said that five sounded better than six.' Other jewellers came and went, such as Norma

Above 'The nice thing was the sociability of it all': Jackie Jones, one of the original Five Jewellers in the shared workshop, and (left) her early account books, showing rent was the biggest single expenditure
Right Craft units included sculptor Nadin Senft, Kermessee which made toys and furniture, and Blind Alley which sold window blinds

Watts and Sarah Goldwater, sharing a lathe, kiln and polisher. 'The original idea for craft workshops was a good one,' says David Taylor, 'and it was quite pioneering. Craft centres are everywhere now, but they weren't back then. Whether it would have worked economically I don't know, but it did set an example to others.' At the time there were far fewer jewellery courses and techniques such as casting were expensive. 'Modern jewellers have a lot more scope than what we had,' says Beverley, 'mass production techniques just weren't good enough then.'

The Five Jewellers were housed between Cloud Nine, a waterbed company and the first business to set up shop, and the Three Potters; Caroline Lord, Mark Brooker and Alysun Peebles, all from Camberwell Art School. Caroline had worked for four years as a beach photographer in Skegness and in a garage to raise the money needed for a kiln. Other craft units included Blind Alley, a screen-printing company which received a lot of coverage for the then original idea of making window blinds, and sculptor Nadin Senft who worked in wood, Perspex and bronze, and who believed a studio-workshop was an ideal way to showcase work, when most people were 'shy' about sculpture and thought it was something that belonged in a museum. Another craftsperson was Paolo Lurati who fashioned bracelets from bent spoons and forks. Next to his unit was photographer David Trace, and then Edward and Pauline Paddon, who produced period architectural and

sculptural reproductions. In 1966 *Pathé News* had filmed Edward at work, promising his reproductions were 'perfect enough to fool many experts' and pointing out that many of his goods had already become collectors' items. David Taylor remembers the Paddons and local antique dealer Paddy Walker, as 'very much parent figures to all the younger craftspeople'.

Ivan and Judi Foster also set up shop in the West Yard, with a business called Kermessee which made toys and children's furniture and sold 'fun things' like a 2p plastic fish that, placed in the palm of a hand, assessed a person's level of passion. Ivan, a graduate from Nottingham Art School, remembers, 'I was sat in my workshop one evening when Peter Sellers and Marty Feldman walked in, that's the sort of passing trade we got. They didn't buy anything but we had a good natter.' Beverley recalls the day she looked out of the window and saw American actor David Carradine, then famous for his role as warrior monk Kwai Chang Caine in the TV series *Kung Fu*: 'He was a tall gangly guy and there he was demonstrating a few moves to Paolo and Dick, the blacksmith.'

On 4 April 1973 the *Ham & High* reported that more than a thousand invited guests attended the opening of Dingwalls Wharf. The Mayor of Camden did the honours, and there was then a three-day display of work over Easter weekend as the area opened to the general public, ending with a firework display and a jazz band. 'There were very good craftspeople, potters and jewellers with art school backgrounds and that's why it all took off,' explains office manager Cathy. There was also a gallery, the Jordan Gallery run by Bill Jordan, in the corner of the West Yard 'where you could buy a Hockney signed print for £25, not that I could ever afford one.'

Around fifty craftspeople had now set up shop, and the press reported on the 'pleasant relaxed shoestring atmosphere' where 'at present everyone seems to like each other.' But from the beginning, says Bill Fulford, he was aware of possible tensions between creativity and commercialisation, and it wasn't long before craftspeople came into conflict with Northside. 'Our first impressions were OK,' says David Taylor. 'I remember a meeting, before the workshops even started, and we were promised all sorts of things. But then we found out there were huge plans for an enormous development and instantly there was distrust. The workshops were installed to convince the planning authorities that the place was attractive and to add credence for a planning application. So we jumped up and objected, and we got a lot of public support.'

Antique dealer and owner of the *Jenny Wren* Paddy Walker had also made an offer for Dingwalls Wharf, and his son Roy remembers, 'Northside wanted to level it and build a large office complex, but pending this they opened up shop units in the old stables and warehouses. Having set the scene, they found opposition. People were concerned about the plans and Dad was one of those leading the opposition. He used to teach at the

Dingwalls Wharf was officially opened in April 1973. The West Yard had a 'pleasant, relaxed, shoestring atmosphere'

Working Men's College and he had a vision for Dingwalls as an arts and crafts centre.'

By now the threatened motorway plan had been dropped, after a hard-fought battle by local residents, and Dingwalls Wharf became 'a lively and interesting meeting place', according to Northside, 'providing a valuable leisure and entertainment amenity for the public'. The company was then given a development lease, with Northside funding the development and British Waterways receiving a percentage of rental income up until 1989.

'We got the original lease on the basis of two young guys with a cheeky scheme,' says Bill Fulford. 'When it came to renew the lease, after the motorway plan was dropped, then they wanted to develop it.'

Such was the success of the site, and with so many people wanting space, that Northside argued it made more sense to have retail shops as well as work spaces. The wharf was isolated from Camden High Street and they wanted to 'increase the pedestrian circulation', extend the facilities of the high street, make the site a starting point for canalside walks, and host daytime activities. The idea, therefore, was to turn the wharf into a permanent arts, crafts and leisure centre. Northside hired Richard Seifert, a British Waterways consultant and the architect who had designed Centre Point, one of London's first skyscrapers in the 1960s. His brief was to come up with a redevelopment plan, pulling down old buildings in Commercial Place and expanding, with more craft workshops, two small cinemas, a pub, shops and studios. 'Seifert's original concept was to knock it all down and start again, that's what you did back then,' says Bill, 'but he was a delight to work with.'

Northside argued that it had explained to everyone from the start that they could only offer short leases and that as soon as the motorway plans were known it would be looking for further development. Risk had been inherent from the beginning, and only seven of the tenancies would be inconvenienced. But craftspeople weren't amused and they formed a tenants' association, which in the following years got numerous planning applications turned down. The association argued that 'a lot of concrete and glass' would destroy the feel of the place, and that craftspeople would be squeezed out by higher rents and be replaced by tourist boutiques and souvenir shops.

'When we first started rent was £1 a square foot,' explains Jackie, 'then after a few years it was £2 and we thought fine, we can afford it. Then later they wanted to charge £9, they said that's what retail rent is. We felt we had given the place a name and we'd been used to get people in, and now they wanted to charge retail rent when we weren't retail, we felt kicked out. We were all a bit naïve, then we realised what capitalism was all about. The early days before the market came were interesting, but there was a lot of bad feeling about the market stalls taking business away from us. We used to see our jewellery designs copied, not made as well and sold for cheaper prices. We felt we paid for studio space all year round and were trying to make a living only to see others reproducing it for beer money.' She remembers the tenants' association holding 'secret meetings' on Paddy Walker's floating restaurant, *My Fair Lady,* 'because no one could hear us on the water'.

For Ivan Foster, Dingwalls Wharf changed from being an extension of art school to more of a trading environment, but as he wanted to move into retail, this was fine by him: 'what I learned was that going to Art College was a waste of time, you're better off going to business school, but it was a fun time.' But for most craftspeople, the shift towards retail was unwanted and they furiously opposed development plans. 'We won the first appeal. Then they filed more,' says David Taylor, who became the association's secretary. 'Northside hated us. They wanted more and more square footage.

Top Left The wharf provided 'a valuable leisure and entertainment amenity for the public'
Bottom Left The tenants' association held 'secret' meetings on *My Fair Lady*, Paddy Walker's floating restaurant
Above A view of Dingwalls Wharf today

Perhaps the commercial pressures were too much. Seifert was hugely famous for getting the maximum floor area; he must have seen the possibilities. But in the end we all got a bit tired of fighting.' 'When there is conflict you often end up with a better solution because everyone listens to everyone else,' says Peter Wheeler. 'Life is a moveable feast, things are not set in stone and conflict can lead to a better solution.' From Northside's perspective, even bad publicity was good and thanks to press coverage of the planning applications – with headlines like 'Development threat to artists' colony' and reports that 'London's Craft Community' were refusing to pay rents – the place was becoming well known, and now the famed music venue Dingwalls Dance Hall had opened as well.

3. Dingwalls Dance Hall

In the late 1960s, during a trip to New York, London wine merchant John Armit paid a visit to Max's Kansas City Club, known for its artistic and jet set clientele such as Andy Warhol, David Bowie and Alice Cooper. 'It had a *huge* bar,' remembers John, 'a restaurant and live music and I thought, well London needs something like this, not a private club but open to everyone. At the time it was near impossible to get a civilised drink in London after 11pm, pubs that had music closed at 11pm and at concert halls people were thrown out at the end of the show.' A few years later John, who lived in north London, discovered Dingwalls: 'it was a run-down packaging warehouse, empty but for some packing cases, with a sign on the wall saying "T E Dingwalls expert for export."

Peter Wheeler, who had tried to open a disco in Watford when he was sixteen, was already keen to have a music venue at Dingwalls Wharf, but knew it would be controversial in terms of planning, as well as getting licences for alcohol, music and dancing. Along with Bill, he'd approached a number of operators, mainly from the West End, including a man known as the 'King of the Clubs' who arrived in a customised black Mini.

John Armit, who liked the look of the site, had £2,000 to invest, Northside had £5,000, and he was then introduced to Tony Mackintosh, who became his business partner. The four men set up a joint venture company to run the dance hall. 'Apart from Tricia's Café the whole place was derelict and significantly under-used,' remembers Tony, 'there were virtually no neighbours, with a canal on one side and a road racing up the other, and we soon realised that was a huge advantage because we were very noisy.'

But first they needed the space occupied by Wilf Scott, opposite the dance hall's entrance. 'A lot of people were against the idea of a dance hall,' he remembers, 'but we didn't mind, we thought it would bring people in and it would be somewhere to go at night. Tony and John really fought to get planning permission, then one day they came into the pub and told us they'd got it. We said, "great, have a beer". We didn't twig. We

Above When wine merchant John Armit discovered Dingwalls it was a 'run down packaging warehouse' with a sign saying 'T E Dingwalls expert for export'
Right There were virtually no neighbours at Dingwalls Wharf, which made it ideal for a noisy music venue

said, "when are you going to start?" and they said "Monday". "One problem", they said, "you have time left on your lease and it's full of your stuff". So we cut a deal, we would have free entry, free drinks, and a meal with staff as long as we were there. They got us out and they were in the place by Thursday. The free drink nearly killed me by the way.'

The pub where the exchange took place was the Caernarvon Castle, then on Chalk Farm Road and opposite today's Market Hall. 'It was a heavy-duty pub if you didn't know it,' says Wilf, 'on Saturday afternoon you'd have the hit men of Camden Town at one end of the bar and local CID at the other, and this was during a lock-in.'

Architects Tchaik Chassay and Julian Wickham designed the Dance Hall, which opened in June 1973, and in order to have a licence to run until 2am it had to charge an entrance fee. 'The court said it had to be 50p,' explains Tony, 'and we thought that was quite a lot, but it didn't turn out to be.' The bill in the first week included the Average White Band, the Scottish funk and R&B band formed a year earlier, and the venue quickly became renowned for its live acts. Jeweller Jackie Jones remembers seeing Marsha Hunt, who had just been in the rock musical *Hair:* 'she was involved in a paternity suit with Mick Jagger and her first song was: "Daddy was a rolling stone"'.

Some customers, however, were more interested in a bar that was open into the small

Above Dingwalls Dance Hall opened in June 1973; the entry fee was 50p and the bill in the first week included the Average White Band

Left The Dance Hall became renowned for its live acts: a flyer from 1976

hours, and Friday nights in particular could be difficult. 'Opening night was wake-up time to me,' remembers John. 'I was on the dance floor and a friend was dancing a bit too much with his elbows and a guy turned round and clocked him. I said, "what did you do that for? Come here", and he followed me meekly and I told the doorman to throw him out.'

Despite the two men's lack of experience, the hall was an immediate success. 'We were taking a risk,' says Tony, 'we only had a temporary three-year planning permission and we knew next to nothing about clubs. I'd never been the other side of a bar in my life, but I quite often ended up as barman at the longest bar in London.' They hired a music man, Howard Parker (known as H) who booked the bands, and then Boss Goodman, and soon realised they needed sound-proofing. 'We didn't have much control over the bands,' says Tony, 'they started one way and then they turned it up. It was good luck about the location, we hadn't thought it out.'

Dingwalls hosted jazz at lunchtime on Saturdays, and with the right band even Monday nights could be full to capacity. They also sold food, such as steaks, and hamburgers in pittas. However they admit the toilets were dreadful. 'I was far too cheap,' says Tony, 'to bother about those.'

Dingwalls soon attracted regular customers from the world of art and music, such

as David Hockney, Lucian Freud and George Melly. 'There was good music,' says John, 'and it was totally original, London had never seen anything like it. Charlie Watts from the Rolling Stones would sit in and drum regularly, Dave Gilmore from Pink Floyd was there three times a week, the whole band would get up and jam, we had them all.'

Photographer Roger Morton, who was given unrestricted entry, remembers Dingwalls as the best venue in London for new music. 'The music was not the main thing, however. It was a great place to meet people, both old friends and new friends. The beer was Adnams, the great Suffolk brewery, managed by Simon Loftus, a regular punter there. Broadside and Barley Wine was the drink of choice. Lethal. Musicians would be there not just to play, but to enjoy the place. It was low and dark and full of life. I think the grot was designed, and the smells came from the tightly packed clientele.'

The Dance Hall soon had its own logo, a saxophone-playing crow, designed by cartoonist John Edward Barker who worked for the underground newspaper the *International Times*, with a comic strip called 'The Largactilites'. Its editor was Mick Farren whose band the Social Deviants played at Dingwalls. The two men also published comic books, including *Nasty Tales*, and in 1973 stood trial at the Old Bailey on charges of obscenity, the first such trial about a comic book in British history, of which they were cleared. Edward drew a number of regular characters, one of which was the crow, believed by some to have been a caricature of Mick Farren, and which became the Dingwalls logo.

The Dance Hall held audition nights and reggae nights, and had an in-house Thursday night band, Ian Dury & The Kilburns, which later became the Blockheads. Within a couple of years it also become famous for its punk bands. 'I remember walking in one evening and I hadn't quite got my head around punk,' says Tony, 'and there was, to me, a terrible screeching noise coming from the stage. Our music manager was sitting there smiling like mad, and I said, "what are you smiling about?" and he said, "they're fabulous, I just got them and they're doing two more gigs". And I said "tell me who they are so I can remember not to come" and he said, "The Stranglers". He had signed them to do three gigs with us.' The Stranglers, formed in 1974, released their debut album three years later, one of the biggest selling albums of punk Britain, which included 'London Lady' and a reference to Dingwalls – 'Little lady/With Dingwalls' bullshit' – in the first line.

Roger Morton remembers many hair-raising nights. 'When Blondie appeared for their debut in the UK, the atmosphere was electric. Debbie Harry exuded such rampant sexuality

Left Inside Dingwalls Dance Hall: 'low and dark and full of life', with the longest bar in London
Above The Dingwalls logo, a saxophone-playing crow, was designed by cartoonist John Edward Barker

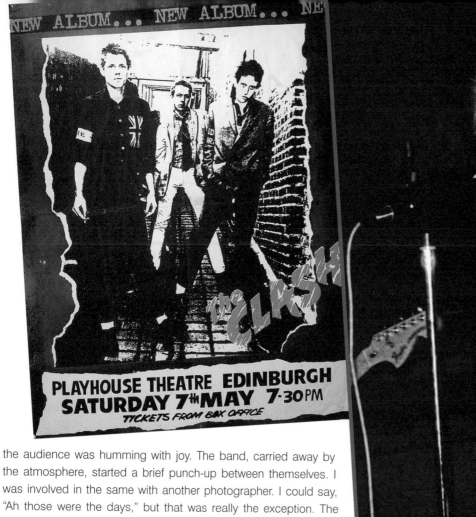

PLAYHOUSE THEATRE EDINBURGH
SATURDAY 7th MAY 7·30 PM
TICKETS FROM BOX OFFICE

the audience was humming with joy. The band, carried away by
the atmosphere, started a brief punch-up between themselves. I
was involved in the same with another photographer. I could say,
"Ah those were the days," but that was really the exception. The
balance between having a good time and going over the top was
carefully controlled, without the punters feeling bad about it. The
great American blues musicians were given a respectful and joyous
reception. B.B. King, Muddy Waters and Bo Diddley were all really
close to the audience both physically and musically. Then there was

the extraordinary George Melly, smoking and drinking his way through his set, never taking himself seriously but wowing the audience nonetheless, and the very original Carol Grimes, always on the verge of breaking through to the mainstream, and given plenty of encouragement by Dingwalls. The atmosphere and the excitement of being there is hard to describe.'

Craftspeople in the West Yard often worked in the evenings and had a free pass to Dingwalls, arguing they needed access to a toilet. Jeweller Beverley Phillips remembers wandering into the Dance Hall one day. 'It was dark and a bit smelly from the night before. I got inside and there was Bo Diddley on the stage rehearsing and I stood there, lurking behind a pillar, listening, and I thought, wow, this guy is a legend.'

'When Dingwalls was good it was absolutely fabulous,' says Tony, 'when it was bad it was dreadful. You've got to be pretty stupid to do something like that. But I learnt an enormous amount about how to run a business and the whole gaboosh of licensing, and we learnt to keep hold of money.'

With Dingwalls Wharf home to a variety of craftspeople and a successful dance hall, it would now become the site of another unique project, an open air Saturday market.

4. The Birth of the Market

On a brisk spring day in March 1974, a young silversmith called Sarah Jones heard some interesting news: a new Saturday market was opening in Camden Town. 'I think someone at *Time Out* told me, and I thought well, brill. I rang a number and said can I book a stall? And they were delighted and said "You're the very first person to ask for one!"'

Originally from Shropshire, Sarah was living in London with her boyfriend Eric Reynolds. She was twenty-two and had only been a silversmith for a couple of years, working part-time as an arts officer for Greater London Arts. But she knew a golden opportunity when she saw one. 'On 30 March I rocked up at this dingy place to find an empty yard. There were sixteen people on the first Saturday, including a couple of other jewellers, which made me a bit disheartened. But I made £20 the first day, selling stud earrings and rings, and I was over the moon.'

Sarah had been given a stall – at the cost of £3 – in what would become known as Park Lane, just behind the railings on Camden High Street. Her stock ranged from 60p twist rings to a £30 sugar bowl, and her neighbours included a couple who sold clogs made in Yorkshire, a man selling hand-dyed duvet covers, and a potter. For Sarah and for many other stallholders, it was the beginning of a major success story. 'For every £2 I made I saved £1, and by the age of twenty-eight I had saved enough to buy a house. Camden Lock Market was a goldmine and it was my life.'

London's original markets had been built back in Roman times, but it was the Victorian era that saw a boom in hawkers and peddlers, who roamed the city during the week and congregated in market areas at the weekend. 'The street-sellers are to be seen in the greatest numbers at the London street markets on a Saturday night,' reported social historian Henry Mayhew in 1851; 'here the working–classes generally purchase their Sunday's dinner.'

By the 1890s there were over a hundred markets in London, including one on Camden High Street, which had started around 1860. However, when traders were accused of obstructing traffic and removed, they relocated to Inverness Street where a small market still exists today.

Silversmith Sarah Jones: 'Camden Lock Market was a goldmine and it was my life'

At the 'Brill' at Somers Town, a mile or so from Camden Lock, trading continued right through the night and into the early hours of the morning. It was more of a fair than a market, according to Mayhew, and virtually impassable after pay time on Saturday night. Hundreds of stalls offered everything from haddock and turnips, pears and baked chestnuts, to new tin saucepans and gaudy tea-trays. On Sunday morning it was full of traders bellowing out their wares – walnuts and apples, combs and braces – until finally the clock struck eleven, 'policemen in their clean gloves' arrived to drive the street sellers out, and Sunday's rest began.

When Camden Lock Market began in 1974, many of the city's markets had closed. In 1964 *The Observer* listed just four markets of note – Caledonian, Camden Passage, Leadenhall and Portobello. There were only four other markets in north London; Chapel Market which started around 1870, Hoxton Market which had its roots in Shakespeare's day, Bell Street, and Camden Passage, which started in the 1960s. There was also a small market of around fifteen stalls on the pavement outside the Roundhouse, a former steam-engine repair shed and then a Gilbey's Gin warehouse, which became an arts venue in the mid-1960s.

Northwest London had more markets on offer, including Church Street and Queen's Crescent, both with Victorian roots, Swiss Cottage, Chalton Street and Kilburn Square. Very few London markets opened on a Sunday, however, and those that did tended to end around midday, like Brick Lane, Columbia Road and Petticoat Lane. But now, as Sarah Jones discovered, there was a new market in town.

On 30 January 1974, Northside had finally received temporary one-year planning permission to use the East Yard of Dingwall's Wharf as a Saturday antique market. Initially it would run just through the summer, with permission for around sixty stalls in the yard and in a corrugated iron structure that became known as the black shed. On day one there were around twelve stalls, but by the end of the summer this had more than doubled to thirty.

Helen Scott Lidgett was another of the first stallholders, then in her early twenties and teaching art at Camden School for Girls. 'Someone told me there was going to be a market while developers were waiting for planning permission. So I went down there with a few bin liners of old clothes, we didn't use the word vintage then, and I thought there would be a queue and there wasn't. There was nothingness, just railings and sloping tarmac and a few tables. But having sold one or two things for a ridiculous amount on the first day I thought, this is great.'

Helen was one of the earliest clothing sellers, a product that the market would eventually became famous for. 'I'd always been obsessed with clothes, great aunties', and old grannies' clothes, I just liked them and I had a glut of Victorian nighties that were very popular.' Twice a month she would get up at 5am and drive three hours from north London to a reclamation or 'shoddy' yard near Dewsbury in Yorkshire, where 'women wearing cross-over overalls sat at conveyor belts sorting clothes from rag and bone men and jumble sales into different fabric categories. This was way before recycling. It was £1 for one-pound weight of clothes, and then you gave the lady a tip as well. It was amazing stuff like chiffon tea-dance dresses cut on the bias. A chiffon dress doesn't weigh anything at all, and we had a pound weight of them. I could sell dresses for up to £50. It was the most unbelievable profit I've ever made.'

Helen soon became a permanent stallholder, and started making her own clothes. She later had a workshop

above Dingwalls, where she made Labour MP Tessa Jowell's wedding dress for her second marriage to David Mills, as well as stalls at Kensington and Portobello Markets. 'I'll never forget that first golden summer at Camden Market when everyone thought it would soon end. It was laid back and friendly, slow and mild. There was a real sigh of relief when we heard the site wouldn't be knocked down because of the motorway, people spread out, and it all escalated.' When Helen's daughter Holly was born she sat her in a buggy under the clothing rails, 'and at the end of the day all the stallholders went to the Hawley Arms for a drink. It was only later on that there was crime and a few rows.' The Hawley Arms on Castlehaven Road, dating back to the early 1900s, became the pub of choice among market stallholders.

Clothes seller Sylvia Keogh was also at the market from day one. 'I saw an ad in a newspaper, I'd been collecting clothes from charity shops and with my partner Terry we had a stall at Portobello Market; we thought we would do both but we settled for Camden. There were quite a lot of nice middle-class young people making toys, jewellery, and leather belts, and then there were people like us, with vintage clothing. People made scarf dresses; they were very hot and trendy then. But the first few weeks there was hardly anyone there; we were all buying from each other. The shops on the high street were full of cardboard boxes; most were boarded up, except the pawnshop.' Sylvia had a large double stall outside the black shed. 'I would buy something for 40p and sell it for four pounds and blush with embarrassment when I took the money. We sold 1930s dresses and Victorian clothes. I used to read *Vogue* and see what was coming into fashion, like Harris Tweed, and go out and find it. People came to spy on us to see what we were selling. All the stallholders were dressed up to the nines; you had to look good to sell things.'

Far left A poster assigning Sarah a stall, she was known to her friends as Sally
Left above Sarah's stock ranged from 60p twist rings to a £30 sugar bowl
Left bottom Clothing seller Sylvia Keogh, clutching a hot water bottle

'I'll never forget that first golden summer at Camden Market': traders outside the Hawley Arms, then the pub of choice for stallholders. Helen Scott Lidgett is fourth from left in the front row

Marc Gerstein, a decorative glass specialist, similarly applied for a stall the weekend the market began. Originally from Connecticut, he was twenty-six and had only been in England for a couple of months. 'I was looking for a place to establish myself in London. I looked at St Katharine Docks, which was years away from being ready, and at Camden Lock which was ready to roll. I showed up and it was all very informal, just a collection of stalls with ropey canopies, cables with electric lights and hammered-together trestle tables.'

Marc made glass lampshades in his bedroom during the week, brought them to the market and priced them at £15. 'I sold constantly, two or three a day. It was encouraging; it was the first time I'd sold anything.' He then moved into a craft workshop with brother and sister Nigel and Rachel Waller, Maggy Granger and David Tomkins of Quayside Antique Restorers. Nigel and Rachel restored furniture and rocking horses, while Maggy made slip-cast dolls' heads. 'I asked if I could join them,' says Marc, 'they gave me a bench and said, "there you go". It was above Dingwalls and very central to the market and this was my key from being a stallholder to having my own shop.'

Marc later moved to another workshop, selling stained glass windows, Tiffany lamps and art nouveau mirror frames. 'It was hard work but it was one big social group and we did things together. Everyone was supportive, people were living a 60s life in the 70s. I got amazing contacts, builders and architects, and I got commissions. It wasn't so much about what you were selling but the people you met who helped you on your way.'

He shared the space with three others, including leather-worker David Bristow and jeweller John Scott, who carved ivory with a dentist's drill, and over the coming years the group expanded until they had the whole upper floor.

David Bristow had started with a stall in the market soon after it opened. He'd been making belts, shoulder bags and wallets for several years and selling them to shops at Kensington Market and at rock festivals. 'It was happenstance,' he says. 'I was with my friend John Scott and we were walking through a street market one day and he saw someone selling scraps of leather. He bought them and turned them into drawstring

pouches, and I followed suit.' When the market opened, David, who had a law degree from Edinburgh, was working at an insurance office in London where he was 'fed up with the lifestyle', and when John got a stall at Camden, David did as well.

To begin with trade was slow. 'I remember a Saturday in February and there was three inches of snow on the ground and I looked around and saw there were more stalls that customers.' But then a leather worker in a second-floor crafts unit asked him to look after his workshop for a year while he went to Australia, and when he didn't come back David inherited it. 'I was sceptical about being upstairs, there were no walkways, the entrance was on the other side and there was a grim-looking set of stairs. For a goodly while I kept both a stall and the shop.' But then he dropped the stall and began supporting himself by making customised items, such as 'a bag for someone who played his trumpet like Dizzy Gillespie' and a doctor who did rescue work around Dartmoor on a motorbike and wanted a bag that could rest on the pillion and hold an oxygen cylinder.

With several stallholders now in place, Northside appointed a new market manager, Eric Reynolds, Sarah Jones' boyfriend. Eric would become synonymous with Camden Market, the most revered – and sometimes feared – man at the Lock. 'Sarah introduced Eric to us,' remembers Peter Wheeler. 'He was good at promotion and laying out stalls. If the market was a stage set then you could say Eric was the lead actor, Bill was the producer, and I was the director. It was the team of three of us that made the Lock work, as well as Cathy and many others. It was a complicated family representing many different business interests but with one main purpose.'

Many stallholders remember Eric as 'the man who got things done'. When the market opened for example, the towpaths on the Regent's Canal were still officially closed to the public, so in order to make the market more accessible Eric decided to make a hole in the wall. 'There was a gate in the West Yard that led onto the towpath, British Waterways locked it at night and didn't necessarily open it in

Left June Carroll ran The Stall, the only food outlet at the market: 'It was survival time, from one hour to another'
Above The Stall was busy from the moment it opened in the morning
Above right Ronnie Carroll, known as a 'showbiz hell raiser', performing at Camden Lock

the morning,' he explains. 'So I opened an entrance out of the East Yard so people could make a circle. I did it with a hammer, so people could get on and off the canal, which at the time you basically had to have a licence to walk on. Then people could circle along the canal, walk into the market and out again.'

Soon afterwards, and following a concerted campaign by the Regent's Canal Group, the towpath from Camden High Street to London Zoo was opened and declared 'a huge success'. While the Regent's Canal no longer carried commercial trade, aside from summer sightseers on pleasure boats, now there would be goods from far and wide sold virtually on its banks, and it soon became a fashionable place to go.

Marice Cumber remembers visiting the market as a fourteen-year-old. 'I first heard about Camden Market in *Vogue*: there was a feature with a very stylish person, she looked very chic and she said she had bought her top hat at Camden Market and I wanted to look like her! There were just a handful of stalls then and most of the area was deserted, but the button stall was amazing, with buttons in the shape of everything, such as beautiful strawberries, and there was an army surplus stall in the corner.'

Camden Lock also became known for its unique food outlet, called The Stall, set up by June Carroll. She'd arrived back in London in 1973 after a year running a hotel in Granada, initially with her pop singer husband Ronnie Carroll who was known as a 'showbiz hell raiser', along with Sean Connery and Stanley Baker. 'I'd sold my house in Highgate to go to Granada,' explains June. 'Ronnie left after six months and returned to England, and I came back at the end of the year penniless with five children; the youngest were three and one. I moved to Sussex and lived in a gardener's cottage belonging to a friend of my husband's. I looked around and thought, what am I going to do to keep body and soul together? I really missed London, I'm a Londoner born and bred.'

In early 1974 she came up to the city for the day and 'wandered around and for some reason I walked down Chalk Farm Road. I was just sightseeing really. Then I stopped at a newsagent's to buy a paper and I saw a notice in the window saying "market stalls opening shortly, please apply" and I thought, I'll apply. So I made a phone call and said I was interested and someone said come in two weeks.'

A fortnight later, she pitched up in a borrowed mini. By then she'd made friends with Sussex landlord Ken Boulter, who ran the pub the Six Bells, and had started to cook for him. He took her to local markets where she bought suitcases of junk for a pound from house clearances, including tarnished silver teaspoons, stained mugs, chipped plaster ornaments and eggcups. She also discovered treasures, like a Victorian ostrich egg mounted on a filigree silver base. So June polished up her goods, and headed to Camden Lock, where she stood dutifully in line with other traders before shuffling off to her allocated stall. 'I stood there, with no idea at all about how a market worked. I put prices on my things, like £3 and someone said "I'll give you £1" and I said "no, it's £3". By the end of the day I had sold nothing, not even the Victorian egg. But I went back.'

June had noticed one stallholder who'd been very successful that day: 'He worked from the black shed, serving customers hot drinks from a hole cut in the outside wall. He wore a dirty apron and he had a spoon tied on a piece of string around his waist, and he stirred your cup of tea with that. And I thought, I've run a hotel, I can do this. Eric said, "OK, you'll need electricity, water, shelter, give me two weeks."' When she returned, the man, apron and spoon were gone. The hatch now led into a storage space, equipped with a tap. There were two six-foot trestle tables, a tarpaulin stretched overhead, and electricity leads dangling down to give power to a kettle and griddle for sausages. 'I had a supply of Sussex sausages, which were fresh with great taste, and I'd gone to a local baker's on Camden High Street and found pitta, which was a wonderful thing, and I thought I'll put sausages in half a pitta and sell them. And that started it.'

June got her eldest children to help, and in the first few weeks Ken from the pub drove her up on Saturdays at 6am. 'It was survival time, from one hour to another. We were always so busy from the moment we opened at 8.30am. It wasn't a stall you could leave, so I trained myself never to go to the loo and didn't drink at all during the day. I had the monopoly, I was the only food stall and if people resented that they didn't dare say it.' June ran the busiest stall at Camden Lock, and many others were quick to follow in her footsteps, starting out from humble beginnings and rapidly building up successful businesses.

5. The Market Takes Off

As Camden Market took off, the first major problem was who would be allowed a stall, and that's when the rows began. 'People could only get a permanent stall if they sold the right stuff,' explains Eric. 'We didn't want fifty people selling skull and crossbone rings or thirty people selling wrist-watches. Very early on there was a man selling Nescafé and general ghastliness and we thought, no, that's not the style we want.' Instead the aim was to offer stalls to people selling unique items, either handmade or imported. 'One man went to Afghanistan and returned by train with carpets on his back; two young women went to the Andes and bought fingerless gloves. People either made things themselves or found an interesting place to bring them from. This was the days before designer and brand names. A lot of people had other lives, they were actors and artists, and they wanted a way to earn a living.'

The queue for stalls started before dawn; people often went to the nearby Hawley Arms until 11pm and then slept in their cars for the night. When Eric arrived there would be sixty people waiting, in wind, rain and snow. 'It was all a bit unkind and silly really. There were fist fights, and people paying others to guard their place in the queue. It was not as friendly as it could have been; there was clearly an opportunity for conflict and it wasn't very civilised. So we came up with a lottery, wrote down names, tore up the paper and people drew the names from the hat so we couldn't cheat them; it was a bit like a lucky dip.' Eric soon refined this method: there were too many similar things being sold so he started to seed the list. 'If you were selling interesting things you went into "A" stream and usually got a space; if you were selling t-shirts then you went into "B" stream and so on. People got upset, not with the system, but because they weren't on the list they wanted.'

Many early stallholders remember people falling out if they had the same goods and didn't get the spot they wanted, or if a competitor sold the same things for less. 'Eric was tough, he had to be, and he did upset people,' says Sarah. 'One chap even kidnapped our dog, a red setter called Thor. He disappeared and we put up wanted posters and a man rang and said "I've got your dog", and all because Eric had told him he couldn't have a stall! We paid him £250, probably stupidly. And then he did it again

Queues for stalls began before dawn. Market manager Eric Reynolds keeping an eye on things

From left Huffs restaurant on Chalk Farm Road; Early morning customers at The Stall'; 'Sunday mornings soon became wild'; Ronnie Carroll helps out at The Stall

and we didn't pay but we got the dog back. He never came back to the market again.'

There were other dramas as well. Architect John Dickinson remembers the day Eric spotted a corpse in the canal. 'He called the cops and they came over. He gave them a boat hook and the Kentish Town constable poked at the body disgustedly. Then the sergeant used the hook to push it to the other side of the canal…and called St Pancras police to tell them there was a corpse on their patch!'

A year after the market started, and despite a general retail ban on Sunday trading, Northside were given permission to operate on Sundays and bank holidays as well. 'When management suggested running on a Sunday everyone said, "It will never work, what a stupid, stupid idea,"' remembers David Bristow. And to begin with, it proved hard getting people to venture along Camden High Street on a Sunday, in the days when all the shops were shut. 'The first Sundays were very difficult,' says Eric. 'I bought newspapers from Steve the newsagent opposite, I thought if the stallholders had something to read and to keep them amused they might stay there. The street was empty, we were the only thing. We would struggle to get people up the road from the tube. There were dreadful days when there was no public at all, sometimes because of the weather.'

However, by the end of 1975 there were about forty-five regular stallholders, and the shift to Sunday trading radically changed life for some traders, like June Carroll who now

worked all weekend. 'My husband was a close friend of Bruce Forsyth and he asked if I could stay with him on the Saturday night, he had a house in Totteridge then, so I didn't have to travel back to Sussex. I packed up the car, stopped at Brucie's and dropped off some of the stuff and came back on Saturday night. On Sunday morning I took all the gear out of his fridge and went back to the market.'

By now, at The Stall at least, Sunday mornings were wild. 'One day there was this guy standing there with a stopwatch. He clicked it every time I had a customer. He didn't buy anything and I thought it was a bit strange but I was too busy to really think about it. The next Sunday he was there again and I asked what he was doing. He said, "I can tell you your turnover, it's impressive." I said, "I don't need a stopwatch to tell me that, I know it is". Then he said, "I own Hampstead Antique Emporium and we have a hayloft, you could open a café there". I said "I'm knackered enough as it is". But I went to see it and I fell in love with it.' June turned the loft into a restaurant called Mother Huffs after 'a real Mother Huff of Hampstead who ran the Mother Huffs Tavern in the early 1700s and who supplied the best cheesecake in London', and later opened a restaurant in Camden simply called Huffs.

Camden Lock also became known for its two on-site restaurants, Lock, Stock and Barrel, described in the press as 'posh', and which in the mid 70s served a table d'hôte

Left Le Routier was a 'crude wooden shack' but attracted customers like Paul McCartney
Right Market customers 'spent hours going through racks of clothes and haggling down the price of a jumper'

dinner for £3.25, and Le Routier, which was open at lunchtime. 'It was a bit crude,' remembers Cathy Palmer, 'just a wooden shack really, but you could park there at night. They had customers like Paul McCartney and excellent food and wine.' But other traders had a hard time selling food in the market. 'My granddaughter Susie wanted a stall to sell cakes,' remembers Jack Whitehead. 'She was fourteen and she and a friend thought they would make cakes and sell them. She didn't realise the market people were quite choosy about the people they wanted, and they kept on putting them off. By lunchtime she'd eaten most of the cakes and gave up.'

But other young businesspeople thrived, and they found Camden Market a good testing ground for what people wanted. 'Once I found a whole chest of coral beads among pieces of broken up Victorian jewellery in a stone shop,' says Sarah. 'I bought ten for tuppence and put on silver backs to make them into earring studs and they looked so pretty. They took a second to make and I sold them for £2 a pair. When people put them in their ears I thought they looked like they had a wart, but customers loved them. I went back and bought the whole chest for £6.' On the downside, she once put all her stock on the roof of her Morris truck at the end of the day, drove off and lost the lot. 'Eric taught me

how to work, how to really work,' says Sarah. 'We worked from 5am, when we put up the stall covers, to midnight and at the end of the day we took down all the covers and banked the takings. We counted all the money and on Saturday and Sunday nights put it in the bank safe deposit in Camden Town. It was thousands of pounds in cash.'

Within a couple of years the market had a wider range of stalls, with antiques, home knitted clothes, £2 silk batik scarves, and hand-crafted mugs for 55p. It was now becoming known for its array of street styles. 'Mods, rockers, skinheads, goths, rockabillies – everyone could find their particular fashion,' remembers Jack. 'People spent a couple of hours going through the rails of clothes, haggled the price of a jumper from perhaps £15 to £13 and went off well pleased.' One young visitor remembers the market as full of people 'spread out selling sarongs and stuff, not even on tables. Everyone was hippy types. It was quite exciting and different and a little scary. But maybe that was because I was ten years old, on my own and I wasn't supposed to be there.' At the Lock Shop, which sold craft goods on a sale and return basis, customers could commission jewellery, ceramics and knitwear. Other craftspeople sold hand-painted silk cushions, handmade leather goods, handmade games and puzzles, original Victorian fireplaces, and oriental carpets. During the week Eric built yachts and then hoisted them up on a Friday night in the black shed, put the stalls underneath and customers were unaware there was a boat over their head. Jeweller Beverley Phillips remembers Eric having a boat on dry land called 'Esoteric', which was popularly known as 'Is it Eric?' One stallholder came down every Friday from Liverpool on an overnight train, with two suitcases of bric-à-brac. This was Alan Williams, the former manager of the Beatles before

Brian Epstein took over. He sold cups saying 'I'm the mug who gave away the Beatles'. 'He was an absolutely lovely man,' remembers Eric, 'but not the world's best business man.'

By now Camden Market was making a name for itself. The *Evening Standard* declared this was 'the acceptable face of property development', and in 1976 it came joint third in a conservation award run by the Royal Institute of Chartered Surveyors and *The Times*. And if the market had started off with a hippy reputation, it soon became a draw for punks, up-coming musicians and film stars.

Clothing seller Sylvia Keogh remembers seeing Malcolm McLaren and members of The Clash in the summer of 1976. Joe Strummer and Topper Headon briefly sold clothes in the market, and a year or so later Dave Stewart and Annie Lennox had a stall for a few weeks to raise money for their band The Tourists, while market visitors included Zandra Rhodes, Raquel Welch and Julie Christie.

'I remember punks coming down to Camden,' says Dempsey Dunkley-Clark. 'It wasn't a look that started there, but there were cross-overs.' She'd started at the market in 1975. "My partner Michael and me were doing a market in Hull at the university and we went to jumble sales and bought brightly coloured pottery, we didn't know it was art deco. A friend came to visit us in Hull and she said, "You could sell this at Camden Lock, you could buy a house with all this!"' So Dempsey moved to London and got a stall, but 'I gave up on vintage because there were racks of it already' and instead she began designing her own clothes, making use of her training at Handsworth School of Dress Design in Birmingham.

As punk took off, with plenty of gigs at the nearby Roundhouse, more people came to the market and Dempsey was the first to sell Crazy Color, the then product of choice for dyeing hair every colour of the rainbow. At one point singer Roland Gift, who would later co-form the Fine Young Cannibals, worked on Dempsey's stall. 'The market was a big part of my life,' he says, 'when I first came down to London.'

Bookseller Chris Overfield started at the market in 1977, in the days when 'every other stall was a junk stall and the black shed was rat-infested and horrible.' Chris, an ex-art college student, had been coming to Camden from Surrey to go to the Roundhouse on Sundays, 'which is what hicks from the sticks like me used to do. Camden was a rather tragic enclave, it was all very down at heel.' He then started working on a bookstall belonging to Nick Dennys, a nephew of Graham Greene's, who'd been at the market since the beginning.

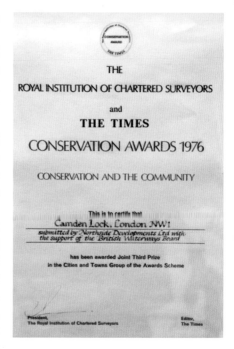

THE

ROYAL INSTITUTION OF CHARTERED SURVEYORS

and

THE TIMES

CONSERVATION AWARDS 1976

CONSERVATION AND THE COMMUNITY

This is to certify that

Camden Lock, London NW1

submitted by *Northside Developments Ltd with the support of the British Waterways Board*

has been awarded Joint Third Prize
in the Cities and Towns Group of the Awards Scheme

President,
The Royal Institution of Chartered Surveyors

Editor,
The Times

One of several awards presented to Camden Lock
Right In the mid 1970s 'every other stall was a junk stall'

Chris remembers several traders of the time; an instrument repair man called Nick, whose customers included English Cricket Captain Mike Brearley, Mike Guest who made a 'potato and pea curry that still makes my mouth water just thinking about it', a junk seller who was 'as mad as a hatter', a man who sold angels taken from Rolls Royces that went for hundreds of pounds, and many people with 'terrifically good eyes for odd stuff. Steve and Ann behind me went to Asia and bought textiles and jewellery and sold beedies, Indian cigarettes. They sold to Liberty and General Trading Company and did stonkingly well.'

When Nick decided he'd had enough of the bookstall, 'he said, "do you fancy doing it as a favour?" and he offered it to me. I thought, "God what have I done?" I sold all the books I had, and then I bought more. But I kind of enjoyed it, it was mad. At the end of the day we all decamped to the Hawley Arms, where the owner Ken would leap over the bar if someone didn't like his beer, which was always dreadful. But it was a fun, buzz pub and a vital end-of-the-day place. Working at Camden Market wasn't about the money but about having a laugh, and I liked the hunter-gatherer aspect of buying and selling.'

Many traders formed firm friendships at the market in the 1970s, commiserating with each other on bad days and looking after neighbours' stalls. 'It was all very jolly,' says Sarah. 'My stall was opposite Angel, she was very funny and sold old linen. One day I had gone to have a pee and when I came back she had put a sign on the felt on my stall saying, "Everything on this stall is a rip off."' Numerous affairs also started at the market. 'It was a good place for picking up,' says one early stallholder. 'There was a lot of flirting and shagging going on at Camden Lock.'

The continuing success of Dingwalls Dance Hall added to the Lock's lively atmosphere and in 1978 the venue celebrated its fifth anniversary. Tony Mackintosh who had 'a reputation for not recognising famous people' remembers the evening well. 'We had George Thorogood and the Fabulous Thunderbirds and the first night of our big concert was over-packed, it was uncomfortable, we'd let in too many people. So on the second night I said "right, close the door" and I told the manager, "you and me we'll stand by the door and not let anyone in." So there was a knock on the door and I opened it to see a little white man. "I'm sorry", I said, "I absolutely can't let you in". The manager pulled me to one side, opened the door and let him in. "It's Bob Dylan!" he said. My reputation was really enhanced.'

Other acts in the period included Muddy Waters, Dire Straits, Etta James, the Damned, Elvis Costello, Madness, Black Slate, Joe Jackson, UB40, and a virtually unknown support band called U2.

By now the Lock wasn't just known for its crafts, market and music, but for the wide range of outdoor, and often free, entertainment. The first big event had been Peter and Kay Wheeler's wedding reception on 27 January 1973, while the first public event was

Dingwallstars

IAN DURY

a Greek night, organised by Peter and a team, along with a local Greek restaurant whose free food ran out in half an hour. Peter remembers bringing the Grimethorpe Colliery Band to London, 'before they became famous, and just before they were about to perform, the licensing authorities insisted that we tie all the chairs together, which we did just in time for the performance to go ahead, and this was in the days before the onslaught of "Health and Safety"'.

Eric Reynolds then launched a series of public events, such as a summer carnival, with Cockney Night, Greek Night, Nostalgia Night, a brass band competition and a Mad Hatter's Ball, as well as carol singers at Christmas. 'We had open-air-canalside dances and got an extension of Dingwalls' licence so people could drink outdoors, which was very unusual then. We closed the West Yard and put down wood so people could dance on a Saturday night, and on

Left Lock founders Peter Wheeler (left) and Bill Fulford on Peter's wedding day in 1973. Bill was best man
Above Dingwalls' acts included Ian Dury, Etta James and Muddy Waters

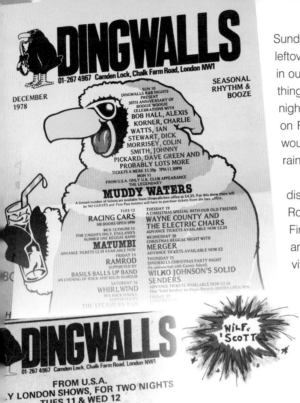

Peter and Kay's wedding reception at the Lock

Sundays we had jazz festivals with the leftover kegs of ale. We were very early in outdoor entertainment; we did unusual things like cooking goats for Caribbean night. But it was hair-raising, because on Friday afternoon we never knew if we would get the licence or not, or if it would rain, and if it did rain we just carried on.'

They also held numerous firework displays, first organised by Reverend Ron Lancaster, founder of Kimbolton Fireworks, in the days before regulation and when people could let off fireworks virtually anywhere. It was then that artist Wilf Scott, who'd arrived at Hampstead Road Lock by boat in the early 70s, forged a new career. He took over the firework displays, along with engineer and cartoonist Tim Hunkin, who later created the Channel 4 series *The Secret Life of Machines*. One of Wilf's first firework displays included a dragon attached to a canal boat that entered Dingwalls Wharf from the Regent's Canal in the dark, throwing out fire.

At the end of the 70s Dingwalls Dance Hall installed a new dance floor, 'luxurious' seating, 'carpeting so deep you'll get lost in it', and 'the most impressive deal yet to go down in a London rock venue – a four screen video system'. It also began advertising its proximity to the market: at the Saturday jazz sessions there was 'no charge on the door, hot food available, booze is cheaper too! Coincides with Camden Lock Market. What more could one wish for?'

Jeffrey the Barak, a member of the Steve Brown Band, remembers the Lock on summer days in the late 70s as 'a charming and enchanting place. Its industrial past was long gone and the area had Dingwalls, and the adjacent market. Our band was from Newcastle so any London gigs felt special, but the people there were nice. They knew how to have a good time at a rock gig and it was relaxed and peaceful, no need for bouncers or security.

The music scene then fused rock, jazz, latin, reggae, folk. It was the 70s and London was hot. The market was mellow and had lots of things that you didn't really need. There was bric-à-brac, hippy gear, cool printed t-shirts. I don't remember seeing any necessities in that market, but it must have been a pleasant hangout for the locals in summer. Something about water in a city, even a generally disused goods canal, creates an atmosphere. Camden Market looked nice and it seemed a million miles from the busy road on the other side.'

But as with all open-air markets, things weren't as pleasant in winter. 'In the summer it was great, on a sunny Sunday it was a bit slow motion with people going past the stall,' says silversmith Sarah. 'But on cold days I sat with a paraffin stove, having hauled my showcases to the market, and I sat there painfully through the winters. God the boredom! Some days it was so cold you didn't want anyone to buy anything because that meant taking your hands out of your pockets. I did people-watching, smoking, and drank endless thermoses of hot drinks. There were lots of days, in the rain and snow, when I took practically nothing.'

Sarah began to keep detailed account books, in which she noted commissioned items like the wedding rings she made for newsreaders Jon Snow and Anna Ford (who didn't in the end get married), and she always made a careful note of the weather – which was often freezing, icy, damp, wet, cloudy, or snowing. On a sunny Saturday in May she could make £162; a week later it was pouring with rain and she only made £30. Despite the winter months, the run up to Christmas was always a good time for trade. On one freezing cold Saturday in December she made nearly £300; two weeks later she only took £14. And then there was the day her sales stopped completely. 'Two dogs were copulating and stuck together in front of my stall. Someone had to throw a bucket of water over them.'

Weather and fluctuating sales aside, theft was another problem. Sarah remembers a group of boys who used to come round and

'Some days it was so cold you didn't want anyone to buy anything because that meant taking your hands out of your pockets': silversmith Sarah and (right) pages from her account books

RINGS.

No.	£	DESCRIPTION.			
100	4	Silver ring with agate. *Stolen*		1	
101	4	" " " sodelic	1	1	1
102	4	" " " agate	1	1	1
103	6	Cast silver rings.	1	1	1
104	15	ring with amethysts	4	4	4
105	35.	22ct ring with sapphires.	1	1	1
106	60p	Twist rings.	1	1	1
107	60p	Loosely twisted rings	42	39	80
108	£2	Plain round bands	9		
109	£3	3 section plain ring.	8	8	8
110	£12	large silver ring. *Stolen*	1	1	1
111	£6	ring with black bullseye	1	1	
112	£5	ring with mother of pearl	1	1	1
113	£6	ring with turq with flower	1		
114	£6	ring with moss agate	1		
115	15	ring with Cornelian	1	1	
116	£15	Set of 5 rings	1		
7	15	" " 5 rings	1		
8	12.5	" " 4 "	1		
	7.50	" " 3 "	1	1	
	10	" " 4 "	1		
	10	" " 4 "	1		

APRIL 12 TH 1975 :   CHEQUES. £61
                     CASH.   £48 - 50
ARKET SALES : — £3 .   109 50

DSC WITH BLOOD GROUP ENGRAVED £5 —
KNOT RING .   - 50
Gilded flower .   £6 - 50
ten ring, agate ring, 2 twists.   £5 - 50 d.
                                      50 .
Twist ring   £3 - 50 d.
earrings - hoop with corals .   £4 — d
Ring with Cornelian .   £2 —
Ring with coral   £48 —
18ct white gold wedding.   £3 - 50
2 plain bands —   £2 - 50

steal. 'They collected their booty in a tweed cap and they put it on an empty stall. Stallholders passed and thought, "hmm, that's mine". So Eric took all the stuff, put it in the cap and marched the boys to the police station. They were just going over the bridge when one of the boys got out a penknife and stabbed Eric in the arm. He was standing there bleeding when one of the boys' uncles drove past and spotted them. He joined in, saying "what do you think you're doing taking my boy?" Eric didn't take them to the police in the end, but we didn't see them again.' Not everyone had success as a trader. Hanne Landin started working in the market in the summer of 1978, and stayed for six months. 'Living around here in the late 70s, it was impossible not to know about Camden Market, it was already very famous. People went there for special things. There was a mood in the 1970s for doing things yourself. Someone said to me, "why don't you try a stall?" So I bought very expensive tiles from Italy, for about £1 each, and I hand printed them, fired them in a kiln and had them framed. You could get a casual stall, if you were lucky enough to win the draw. What was ghastly was packing the heavy tiles, taking them down there, unloading them and *not* getting a stall and taking everything home again. I usually got one, though. I suspect Eric slightly kept an eye open for us craft people; he wanted to keep it varied so it was more interesting for people to come to. We were all terribly in awe of Eric. But I wasn't very successful and I never had a big day; I don't know why I bothered. It was mainly young people looking for clothes and jewellery and maybe something to eat, they were certainly not looking to furnish their homes, they were not at that stage of life yet. So I moved to Hampstead community market and did very well, and later I had a stall at Covent Garden, where people had far more money.'

One visitor, Simon Dixon, remembers Camden Lock as 'a kind of hippy heaven. It was 1979, the time of the Iranian revolution and I'd tried to go to India by bus and failed because of Iran and went back to Paris instead, this was the time when you could take a bus to Marrakesh and such. London looked a mess but I was young and smoking my roll-ups and pretty happy. The market was basically just next to the lock, and I don't remember much on the street...except someone selling Dylan bootlegs against the railings outside, in the rain, covered by a sheet of plastic. I remember the smell of burgers, the hard cobbles underfoot, being alone and wide-eyed at it all. I had left Paris by mistake, and was trying to like London, and Camden Lock qualified as home, a zone of sympathy. Well, all of Camden High Street really: the books and records and the cinema, the market was the jewel in the crown.'

The Lock hosted various
outdoor events in the 70s; even
Prince Charles (top right) came
to have a look around

There was always something to see at the Lock in the 70s; events held in the West Yard included canalside music and dances

6. The Lock in the 1980s

Camden Market in the early 1980s was going from strength to strength, with nearly 200 stalls, 100 permanent stallholders, and up to 11,000 visitors at weekends. The Lock's directory, meanwhile, listed thirty-nine permanent businesses, such as Glassworks at 30c, which sold glass and steel furniture by artist Danny Lane. Born in Illinois in 1955, in the 70s Danny had arrived in London where he'd studied painting at Central School of Art. 'I grew up in the Village in New York City in the 60s, when things like leather craft were blossoming, but I found the attitude to craft in England was different; the middle class had a problem with handmade stuff, it was seen as manual work. And I always said, no, it's art.'

After college, Danny worked on building sites to earn money to rent a studio in Hackney. 'I had no practical sense back then, I was totally left-brain. Then around 1981 I met John Creighton, a master glass engineer, and he had a crafts unit at Camden Lock. He was doing customised engraving on glass, like drinking glasses and signs, and we went into partnership and turned it into a shop. I made small objects in my Hackney studio during the week, and then sold them at Camden Lock at the weekend. During the week there was no one there, it was quiet all week but at the weekend the Lock was blistering.'

Rents had now increased to £7 per square foot for studios and up to £5 for workshops, and the tenants' association was again concerned that this would force people out. 'Both John and I had young families and we were struggling to make ends meet,' says Danny. 'The rent seemed high to us, and all of the craft shops found things really difficult, but for me it was a great starting place in a nation of shopkeepers. That's what London is, markets. It's real and you meet the public. I would be in our workshop trying to do these artworks and some big guy with a can of Special Brew would wander in and say, "What's that supposed to be anyway?"'

During the week the Lock was empty; at the weekend it was 'blistering': the Chalk Farm railway bridge before it was re-painted

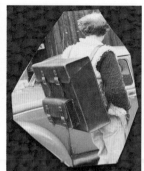

When Danny sold his first major piece of work, a large wall piece for £350, 'it was a miracle for John and myself. Selling that piece encouraged me to experiment with different things and while my ambition was art not making trinkets, one Christmas at the Lock we did try to do something that people would buy. We made thousands of small make-up mirrors and sold them for a few pounds each, they went like hot cakes.'

Danny then decided to make larger, more expensive pieces and after two years he left the Lock and went on to become a glass sculptor of international repute. 'A market is a good testing ground for how to deal with people and to see how people respond to things,' he explains. 'So many successful people have come through markets, barrow boys have a canny sense of how to buy and sell. At the time I would have rather been in a Cork Street gallery, but what I needed in retrospect was that market, and it was at the Lock that I met my great friend Peter Wood who continues to photograph my work to this day.'

Other traders similarly discovered that Camden Lock was an ideal place to experiment with goods and launch new ideas. Leatherworker David Bristow began making stained-glass-patterned belts, influenced by the work of colleague Marc Gerstein. 'I'd had a few drinks one evening and I thought "hang on, what about if I did something with a stained glass ambiance?"' He also designed Spanish and Arabic inspired belts, and continued to make commissioned items such as a bag for a dealer in rare and ancient books. 'He traveled the world and he wanted an unprepossessing scrappy-looking bag so no one

Left Leatherworker David Bristow and examples of his goods; customised bags, hair clips and stained-glass-patterned belts
Bottom left Dick Scowen, a glass specialist, working in the Lead & Light workshop
Above The Body Shop stall was its first franchise to open outside Brighton

would think he had anything of value. The day he collected it, it was raining and he said, "don't look", then he kicked it down the yard to make it look grotty.' David also made a bag for a TV executive who 'wanted something to hold his new fangled portable cassette player', and sandals and shoes, although the former 'could be dodgy if you had a bad summer', as well as hair slides fashioned from scraps of leather.

Other traders included Ray and Barbara Bathke who opened Village Games in a small corner shop in the West Yard in 1982. Seven years earlier they'd launched a large game and toyshop in Hampstead, 'but the rents got out of hand,' says Ray, 'so we sold the lease and came to the market. It was pretty dead in the week, but it was a laid back, hippy market and very enjoyable. There was a very big local population and very few tourists.'

There were now nearly 100 markets in London, just as there had been in Victorian times, as well as two comprehensive guides to the city's market places. 'The idea of making things and selling them at a market is back in fashion,' declared one; '"small is beautiful"' seems to be here to stay. Camden Lock is all very relaxed and pleasantly informal – cobbles, barges, old brick and timber-clad warehouses and tiled roofs.' Goods on offer included hand-painted bread bins, greeting cards, candles, ethnic jewellery, badges saying 'gay whales against racism', and handmade fudge in ten flavours. There was also a Garden Centre called Jennings and a stall belonging to the Body Shop, its first franchise to open outside the company's birthplace in Brighton.

Another market guide described the courtyard at the back of Camden Lock as full of buskers but 'calm and relaxed with a vaguely Parisian air reminiscent of the concourse outside the Pompidou Centre'. It found the second floor workshops 'unique if sometimes twee', and described a 'recent Camden syndrome' which 'throws up images of women in Indian dresses with anaemic-looking babies strapped to their backs clutching whole food rusks; and men with wispy beards and national health spectacles, walking along reading *The Oxford Dictionary of Quotations*.'

Others were more fulsome with their praise. 'On some days an open market operates

in a small area by Chalk Farm Road Bridge,' explained a guide to London's canals. 'This development is an excellent example of the good that can be achieved with a worked-out commercial site which had become an eyesore.'

Northside now decided it was time to change the name of the road Commercial Place to Camden Lock Place. While Bill had initially suggested the site be called King Camden, he and Peter agreed to call it Camden Lock. 'It was a lock and it was in Camden,' says Bill, 'and Hampstead Road Lock didn't describe where it was.' Camden Lock was already in common usage and had featured in Dingwalls Dance Hall promotional material for some years. But the fire brigade objected to the change of name, saying there were too many locations in NW1 which started with the prefix Camden and if someone reported a fire it would be confusing. Northside responded that if someone reported a fire they

Above An elephant crosses Camden High Street: stunts and attractions at the Lock in the 1980s included a performance by Gerry Cottle's Circus
Right Northside commissioned a 32-foot-high mural at the end of the newly named Camden Lock Place

would be certain to say they were in Camden Lock, not the outdated and rarely used Commercial Place.

In fact there had already been a major fire, when in 1980 the former Gilbey's Bottle Store, a four-storey Victorian building that ran the whole length of Commercial Place and was being used as a storage depot, went up in flames. 'It was at night,' remembers Eric Reynolds, 'and I wandered in before the police and fire brigade had closed off the road. I walked into the Northside office and then I was stuck there. I could see the walls starting to fall down, there was the most enormous heat and the steel frame of the building bent like spaghetti.'

The Greater London Council eventually allowed Northside to change the name of Commercial Place, and Camden Lock was marketed widely in the 80s with ever more varied stunts and attractions, including a five-week Festival of Entertainment, a Festival of Clocks, and a performance by Gerry Cottle's Circus held on the derelict site of the old bottle store. There were also coffee concerts, buskers such as Vulcan the fire-eater (who was so popular that crowds became a problem), Zippo the clown, and a celebration of Prince Regent's Day.

Posters and flyers were produced, promoting the Lock as 'London's only waterside village', with craftspeople, designers, restaurateurs, music and stallholders. Northside also commissioned a huge 32-foot-high mural, displayed at the end of Camden Lock Place, which featured on the cult children's TV show *Blue Peter*.

'We created an address,' says Eric, 'and we were very inventive. One Christmas we hired TV man

Johnny Ball as Father Christmas, another year it was a man who had been to both the North and the South Pole' – this was David Hicks, a member of Ranulph Fiennes' Transglobe Expedition of 1979–82. Another winter Eric 'borrowed' some reindeer from London Zoo, the press reported: 'The Santas took to oars when the reindeers brought in for the occasion to tow them along the Regent's Canal took fright at the crowds of Christmas shoppers.'

'The things we did, we couldn't have done them now,' marvels Eric. 'We had open-air bronze casting, it was remarkable that we could do that, it was a different world back then. In one event we had people on the roof of the Interchange Building when there were no rails, nothing.' Assisted by Arabella McIntyre-Brown, Eric's events were wildly successful, and he once converted an old empty barge into a swimming pool.

Northside now attempted to introduce new development plans. In the late 1970s it had submitted applications to the council for the permanent use of Camden Lock and the redevelopment of the East Yard. The council refused, Northside appealed and a public inquiry was held in 1980. The following year Michael Heseltine, then Secretary for State, granted planning permission.

Northside was allowed to put up market stalls in the East Yard, although only for three years, and eventually got temporary planning permission to use Camden Lock Place as well. The Council then said it would only renew planning permission if the site were re-developed. 'They got in Seifert,' remembers architect John Dickinson, 'and he wanted to build housing and offices, it was all low key and low rise but Camden refused. He appealed and lost. So I said "can't I do a scheme?" and they said "you're not qualified yet", so I did it on behalf of Seifert, on his drawing sheets. He didn't like mine but Camden was warmer towards it. Mine had no housing, and while it wasn't one of my best, it preserved all the buildings and his didn't.' John's plan was rejected, but he was now a qualified architect and Northside asked him to work on a new scheme, with plans for

Dingwalls celebrated its tenth anniversary in 1983: acts of the period included the Police, here (top left) being mobbed outside the Dance Hall, and (right) Toyah Willcox

two levels of shops on Chalk Farm Road.

In the meantime, Camden Town had become 'an activity area for local people and families', remembers Roy Walker. 'It was popularised by the press and by the pop groups that had played at Dingwalls in the 70s and people came to see where they played.' Dingwalls Dance Hall now employed twenty people full time and another forty part time, most of whom lived in Camden, and was attracting 2,000 people on weekday evenings and 750 during weekend lunch times. In 1982 Dingwalls was sold to Harvey Goldsmith and the following year the Dance Hall celebrated its tenth anniversary as a music venue, known far and wide as the canalside home of Rhythm and Booze. 'While fads and fashions twirl around the fiscal flagpole that is the whacky world of showbiz,' read one of its birthday advertisements, 'Dingwalls has enjoyed and endured a decade as both a music business hangout and a jolly nice place for punters to have their ears massaged.'

Regulars remember it as 'pretty dingy and divey', with black walls and a long sticky bar. It was, reported *The Ham & High*, 'as determinedly unchanging and unfashionable as ever…looking a little out of date and scruffy, but still churning out the music every night. Its crowning glory, the bar, was once where canal ponies were tied up and some may say unkindly that the clientele has not changed much.' While the whole place smelt permanently of beer and the lavatories were 'far from immaculate', it still managed a month of celebrations that ended with Elvis Costello and the Attractions, one of the acts Dingwalls had helped to discover. Others included in the birthday celebrations were Dr Feelgood, Sugar Minott, The Clash and Ian Dury.

Meanwhile, such was the success of the market in the early 1980s that it was now managed by a team, with Eric Reynolds being joined by Alan Jones, as well as several assistants. Alan, a former big yacht skipper then living on the south coast, first met Eric through a shared love of boats. 'He was building sailing boats and I sold him some fittings and worked with him for about four years. He also used to race lawn mowers. At the weekends he worked at Camden Lock and he said to me one day, "I'm not coming down on Monday; I'm handing over the boat business. Why don't you come and work with me at the market because god knows I need some help up there".' So Alan came to London, took up residence on a boat just 100 yards from the market, and was given jobs such as painting the office. He then started collecting rent as well, which was now £7 per stall.

At the time the market operated on 'a two-thirds one-third profit share basis,' explains Eric. 'I ran and promoted the enterprise on the land Northside leased from British Waterways. I collected the rent, direct costs were deducted and the surplus income was split two-thirds to Northside and one-third to me. Our interests were therefore aligned as it was to the general benefit to grow the market and to contain costs. In the early days the weekend "workforce" was just myself and a sweeper.' As the market grew there were more hands-on staff, sweepers, stall erectors, assistant managers, and event organisers. One sweeper, a poet and musician, supported his art through his wages and is now a university professor. 'Over the years the market offered thousands of opportunities for employment and small business start-ups,' says Eric. 'Many of the people were quite exotic and spun off into all sorts of wonderful futures. To promote new market days we put on "attractions". One Boxing Day we put on a surreal play called "The revenge of the Christmas Pudding" which amazingly gathered a crowd.'

Alan remembers that people 'feared and revered Eric, but he's actually quite a shy person. He was hard working, focused, dynamic and creative.

HE LOCK — BEFORE AND AFTER

Dingwalls Wharf — "unlovely, but with potential"

swan through the stubby grey
of the ugly duckling took some
and lots of imagination. The
ave been implemented over a
time, so that the character of
torian buildings has been
ed, whilst turning the
es, stables and timber yard into
sent community of craft
ps, restaurants, design studios,
y and weekend market.
its inception, the Camden Lock
as been attractive to the smaller,
pased businesses, and the
has been carefully balanced to
interest and variety both to
and the community working

Camden Lock is an example of what
can be achieved without major
expenditure or government inter-
vention. The recent development of the
area has been evolutionary — with each
change or improvement creating a new
point of departure for the next stage in
the development.

From the busy horse-powered days of
the early 1800s, when the canal carried
everything from coal to wine, through
the changing fashions and fortunes of
transport and industry, Camden Lock
has been an important centre of activity
in the area — until the 1960s, that is,
when Camden Lock became a backwater. Since the early 1970s, however,
the refurbished and rejuvenated site has

become the new heart of this part of
London, and has turned the tide of
fashion in a most effective way. The
canal is used commercially once more,
the boats now carrying passengers rather
than freight. The area in general has
received a substantial boost in terms of
employment and architectural
renovation, with a number of high-
quality retail businesses and media-
related companies (notably TV-am and
Design House) coming to the area.

Camden Lock will no doubt continue
to change and develop with the years,
but will always maintain the character
and atmosphere of the site, remaining
one of the most unique and charmingly
unspoilt sites in central London.

amden Lock — the potential realised

Markets need promotion and that includes self-promotion and Eric was very good at it. I worked for him for three years before I realised it was Bill and Peter who actually owned the market!' Alan quickly had to get used to tensions over who would get a stall 'It was competition for a good space, that was the critical factor. We wanted quality stock to be more easily seen and to give an opportunity to a young trader straight out of art college who might go on to really make a name for herself. The site always had a very high proportion of creative, single-minded women making their way in a slightly unconventional environment. By contrast many of the male traders appeared to be marking time until something better turned up… perhaps in their acting career or if their band hit the big time. We rarely turned people away and I tried to put people at ease, providing a service and to do it all with a sense of humour and a touch of theatre, and to make it a relationship between two individuals, not a market manager and a trader. We wanted craft, anything but rubbish, like cheap imported souvenirs, cheap clothing, or cynical people who went to third world countries, bought mediocre stock for third world prices and then came back and sold it for first world prices.'

There were now around 250 stalls at the Lock in peak season; ninety percent were permanent and the rest casual, with potential traders gathering outside the Lock Shop at 9.30am. Many stallholders remember seeing 'grown men cry' when they failed to get a pitch. Alan's response is, 'If any grown men did cry they were victims of their own flakiness. A market runs a lot better if the rules and regulations are for the good of the site. If someone

Camden Lock continued to host events in
the 1980s to promote the market, proof that
the old Dingwalls Wharf had been transformed
into a bustling venue

was late once then we understood, but if they turned up late several times, saying "ah my alarm clock didn't go off" or "I had to get a train," and someone in the queue had quality stock and was on time, then they got the stall.'

'Even if you were a regular, if you didn't turn up on time for your stall then you lost it,' remembers Wendy Shuttleworth. 'People always were whingeing about something, that the power was down, that there were people on their space, that the tarpaulin leaked. This was before mobile phones and people got shirty if they turned up late and found their stall gone but hey, that was their problem.' However Eric Reynolds, at least, had a phone. In the late 70s he'd bought a radio phone, which he carried around in a suitcase, and in the 80s this was replaced by a Vodaphone, to which he was one of the country's first 500 subscribers. 'It was the size of a brick,' remembers one stallholder, 'and no one else had one so I've no idea who he was talking to.'

Wendy had first begun working at the market when she was fifteen. Like a lot of teens she found it was a relatively easy place to get a job. 'It all started when my dad said to us one day, "you kids are costing us too much money, so I'm going to give you pocket money". When he told me how much I said, "stick it; I'll go earn my own money."' So she started selling jewellery on a trestle table outside the Roundhouse and then moved to Camden Market, sharing a stall with a silversmith called Victor. 'We sold all sorts of things like knitted brooches and varnished licorice allsorts, and we sold them for pennies – 35p, 50p – and I spent more money than I made, buying things from other stalls.'

Wendy then moved to a stall by a big red bus on Camden Lock Place, where 'friends who had been up all night would come and sleep under my stall, punk rockers and bikers. An arm would fall out and customers would jump in fright and I'd have to kick my friend back under the stall.' Another famous bus of the time was the Fun Bus belonging to Capital Radio, whose own music festival started at the Lock.

Anna Kusner also started work at the market as a teenager in the early 80s, although her initial aim wasn't to make money. 'I was best friends at school with Sophie Gardner, we were about fourteen years old and we both fancied a boy called Joe Swift who was friends with Sophie's brother and worked at the market. I'd gone around asking stalls for a job, I didn't really want to work at the market, I just wanted to stare at Joe, but we ended up with a job on the badge stall. We got paid £5 a day and we split it because we both fancied Joe and wanted to look at him all day long. The novelty wore off pretty quickly, it was freezing.'

PITTA and SALAD 25-35p

LAFAGNE 50p

BREAD and CHEESE ... 25p

CHOCOLATE CAKE 20p

CHEESE CAKE 20p

FRUIT JUICE 15p

FRENCH COFFEE 12p

TEA 8p

June at work on her stall, where 'people went crazy for the food'

However, market life was a fun way to earn money. 'If you were looking for a Saturday job you went down to the Lock and got one.' Tired of the badge stall, Anna approached June's food stall, 'I asked for a job and they said "yes come back next week." At the end of my first day I got £15, in three crisp five pound notes, and I said "I think you've made a mistake". I was so excited; I took everyone to Hampstead Tea Rooms. The next week I went back and they asked how old I was. I said fourteen. They said "come back when you're sixteen."'

She then started making earrings and selling them on the pavement under Chalk Farm Bridge, 'it did bring out my business skills; I saw the potential to make a killing, and we had a real little business empire going on.' After that it was back to the food stall where she worked every weekend for two years.

'It was busy morning to night. The breakfast menu included things like a croissant and bacon, juice and coffee, the rest of the day there were sausages and hamburgers, we cooked them up on a grill and put them in pitta with salads, like garlic green beans. Food like that wasn't common at all and there were queues right up the street. Fifteen people worked on the stall at one time, and our belts were constantly stuffed with money.' Anna briefly took a Saturday job at the chemist Boots but only lasted two weeks 'because they didn't like the colour of my hair. It was £15 a day at Boots, whereas at the food stall it was £50. It was hard work and the hours were long, from 6am to 7pm with a ten-minute break here and there, but I was living like a queen.'

'People went crazy for the food,' remembers Chris Demetriou, who worked on the stall while studying for a foundation in fine art, 'all the homemade coleslaw and curried rice salad. It sounds silly now, but no one else was doing it and people queued for hours. It was quite exhausting, but fun, with a young crowd who all went to the Hawley Arms afterwards. The pub was a right dive, but all the market traders went there.'

Jacey Sallés also started at the Lock when she was fifteen. 'Everyone wanted a job at Camden Lock, it paid more than at a shop, and after two friends Jill and Julie got work at the food stall, I kept hassling them for a job. After my first day I was "sacked" because

Dani, June's daughter, said I talked too much. But I kept ringing and three weeks later I was told I could come back if I knuckled down.' Jacey worked every weekend from 8am-4pm, her job paying her way through Rose Bruford College of Theatre & Performance. She was then given a later shift, from midday until the end of the day. 'I would go rave all night, get in at 10am, have a shower and head to the Lock. I remember serving Boy George, and Barbara Windsor was a regular at the stall, she'd always say, "a cup of tea darling." I loved the sociability of it, it was the only food tender and I had the most amazing social life. Wind, rain and shine, I just loved it. It was the Dunkirk spirit, it would be crashing down with rain and people had no cover, or the tarpaulin would fill with water and people would prod it with a broomstick and shout, "mind your back!". It was a naughty game people played. In the winter you had frost bite, come summer you made money. The food stall was one of the first places to do a tasty veggie burger, and I enjoyed flirting with people, "Oh boys," I'd say, "you look hungry…veggies only up my end I'm afraid…" But you had to be very quick and you had to beg to go to the toilet, Ronnie Carroll would only let you go if you said you were having a "lady's emergency". He would be behind you almost with a riding crop, saying "faster faster". At 11am, after

Above Chris Demetriou (left) worked on the food stall while studying art; Jacey Sallés (top, far left) used her job to fund her way through drama school
Right June Foulds (second from right) with the British 4x100 metres relay team after winning gold medals at the Commonwealth Games in Cardiff in 1958 and breaking the world record

the morning rush, he would say, "massage time". He had a bad back and I would give him a massage while he went on about the old days and the rat pack.'

Theft was sometimes a problem. One day June was double-parked outside making a food delivery, and Jacey remembers running out 'to get the bread, quiches and big tubs of salads. She'd left the engine running and on the seat I saw a massive bag of change; she'd left the door open or the window down and I told her and she said, "just get the bread through darling." I was walking back to the van when I saw two boys put their hands in and grab the money and run off past the Hawley Arms. You have never seen a woman sprint so fast, they were 200 metres ahead of her and she flew down that road like a comet, screaming at them. The kids saw a fifty-year-old flying after them and they literally dropped the bag on the floor, she picked it up as calm as anything and came back and I was like, "way to go June!" They chose the wrong person to run from.'

What the would-be thieves didn't know was that as a teenager June had been a champion sprinter. In 1950, at the age of sixteen, June Foulds had created history at the European Championships by becoming the youngest athlete to win a gold medal, in the 100m relay. At the Helsinki Olympics of 1952 she won a bronze in the relay, followed by silver in the 1956 Olympics in Melbourne, and she only retired in 1958 after pulling an Achilles tendon in the European Games.

June put her skills to good use more than once at Camden Lock. 'I had a restaurant on Chalk Farm Road and at the end of the day I took the cash there. One day a boy rushed right through, grabbed my handbag and ran. I took off after him. He was bloody fast. I kept going, but I was thinking, I'm a sprinter not long distance. I was plodding after him. But he must have got tired because at last he threw down the handbag and I got it back.'

While many stallholders used their salaries to fund their studies, others spent their income going abroad. Anna Kusner went travelling for four years, coming back to England through

cycled the streets asking youngsters if they would like to join the club. Well, I wasn't there when she got to my road but the kids pointed to our door and suggested she called. Fine, my grandfather said, it'll get her off the streets, and I found myself trekking all the way to Richmond with a sixpence bus fare in my pocket.'

She had no gear but they asked her to race 100 yards and she won, as old Jack Holden says, 'out of sight.' The woman on the bike rummaged around in her daughter's old gear, found a red track suit, an old pair of spikes and a baggy pair of red (the Spartan colours) shorts and a sprint star was born. She sped through the ranks that season but was fired up by a handicap meeting she went to where she was given a ten yards start, won easily and became the owner of a red and white plastic pyjama case. "That got me hooked," she said, "it seemed so easy."

JUNE PAUL setting a UK 200m record of 24.1 in 1956

Bali, and enrolling on a business degree. Then, along with her friend Bella, she decided to raise a lump sum to open a restaurant. 'We got people to invest, went back to Bali and got 10,000 swimming costumes made. We bought them for 15p each and came back to Camden Lock to sell them for £8.50. The first day on the stall I was a bit naïve. I had around £800 in my money belt and stuffed in all my pockets, then I looked down and saw a £5 note floating in the air. Everything I'd earned had been nicked, and I hadn't felt a thing. We didn't go back to the Lock after that.'

While many stallholders were immensely successful in the early 80s, some decided the life wasn't for them. Janet Campbell was in her mid 30s when she first started. 'It was a question of necessity, I had five kids and I needed to make money.' She sold 1930s china, often brought from jumble sales in Brighton, as well as old coats and buttons. She also sold hedgehogs, which were made from teasels. 'They were crafted by an old lady. She dressed them up in clothing as Beatrix Potter characters, and they sold regularly.' Janet experimented with selling things and this developed into an interest in old china: she went on a course and learned how to restore it, and then she'd repaint it and sell it at the market. Eventually she got a permanent stall in the middle row, but it was then that she started having second thoughts, 'I watched how people changed, I didn't like

Sprinter June, who put her skills to good use at the Lock when she ran after thieves, pictured here as a teenager (far left), her knee stained with cinders from the running track

it and I decided it wasn't a career for me. People were quite dissatisfied; there was a lot of moaning and they were always coming up with things to blame for a bad day. I was very good at selling stuff but I felt uncomfortable about getting people to buy things. I felt as if I was conning people. It was the psychology of it all; you would tell someone they looked dreadful in one thing and then great in another and they would buy it. Sometimes I just said, "oh have it." I didn't want to develop that side of myself. And people were very nasty about their clients, saying "there they go walking round without buying anything." The way people developed, it was like the client was the enemy, they'd say, "look at her, she's no intention of buying anything." Trading is the basis of life, it is survival, but if you had a conscience it wasn't easy. I didn't depend on it for a living, so I had a choice and after a few years I left.'

By now many of the original traders from the 70s, such as silversmith Sarah Jones and clothing seller Helen Scott Lidgett, had also left the Lock. Sarah, whose former boyfriend Eric was now married to food seller June Carroll, moved her business to Basinghall Street in the City, 'I took everything I'd learnt in the market with me, and it proved invaluable.' Helen left to open a clothing shop on Chalk Farm Road, called Scots, with a ten-year lease, paying just over £5,000 a year for the shop, basement and access to car park, but such was the success of Camden Lock that her rent increased to £25,000, and she decided to move on. Clothes seller Sylvia Keogh similarly decided she'd had enough: 'lots more people were doing the same stuff, if I couldn't make money there was no point in being there, and the camaraderie had gone.' The Five Jewellers also shut up shop, driven out by rising rents.

Meanwhile Northside had expanded business onto the canal itself. When British Waterways put its zoo Waterbus boat up for sale because it was making a loss, Richard Branson of Virgin fame apparently wanted to buy it, but Northside and Eric Reynolds made a successful offer and bought it as a joint venture. Maggie French began working for the Waterbus in 1986. 'It was by accident, I'd studied environmental science and geography at university, then I'd been working in arts, for theatres and in bars. I'd been on holiday, and I came back looking for a job and Eric got me involved in a music festival. After that, he said "come and work for us." I knew nothing about boats but Steve King was running it and I learned from him.' They now had three boats – *Water Buffalo, Gardenia, Perseus* – and later bought another boat, the *Milton*, a working pottery boat in the Midlands, which they turned into a passenger boat. The boats were repainted in traditional colours and a

Northside expanded business onto the Regent's Canal when they bought British Waterways' zoo Waterbus, later increasing the fleet with the *Milton*, a working pottery boat from the Midlands

regular timetable service was introduced between Little Venice and Camden Lock. 'It was very quiet when I started and there wasn't anything like it,' says Maggie. 'There was no promotion of the canal itself until the 1990s; the towpaths were still locked at night. But people love boats because it's something different, they are small and close to the water and you can talk to the crew so there's the personal touch. For many people it's the only opportunity to go on a canal boat, unless you have the money to buy one.'

Such was the popularity of the market in the 80s, meanwhile, that some young entrepreneurs didn't even bother trying to get a stall, instead setting up shop on bridges and pavements. David Marks discovered the Lock because of the local music scene and was a regular visitor to Dingwalls. 'You'd often see people like Jazzie B and Norman Jay walking through the market. I remember one Saturday afternoon in July I bumped into Norman Jay, he didn't know me but he gave me a nod and he goes, "are you going to see Roy Ayres?" And I said, "where?" He said "Dingwalls". And I said "when?" He said "two minutes". And I went there and it was like a secret gig, it was a fantastic vibe.' David turned his passion for music into a business, making bootleg mix tapes of northern soul, R&B, and rare groove. 'At the time a blank TDK cassette cost 50p. I would make one master copy from the records I already had, and then stay up all night copying it. I'd make

100 tapes and price them at £5 each. I made little covers as well, with cool black and white pictures of boxers like Sugar Ray Leonard, and inside I would write the list of songs. Then I nicked a small card table from my parents' house, just two feet by two feet, and took it up Camden High Street to the humpbacked bridge and set up just there on the left. I wasn't trying to avoid the rent of a stall; it was just the busiest place to be and you didn't need a tarpaulin or anything. I put out a massive beat box with loads of new Duracell batteries, there was a constant stream of people and I blasted out northern soul. There were certain songs, like Sir Joe Quarterman's "So much trouble in my mind" and Marvin Gaye's "Trouble man", that really got people going. No one moved me on; I think they liked the music. There was a guy called Jeff, he sold t-shirts and he would look after me a bit. I would sell out in an hour, I made £500 when it had only cost me £50. I was done.' But one day he got a shock: 'two guys came up and each bought a copy of every tape I had, mainly 70s soul stuff, which had never happened before. So I packed up and walked down to the tube. Then I got stopped by two plain-clothes police officers. I was worried. They told me they knew I'd been selling tapes on the bridge. They said, "do you realize you're in violation of such and such laws" and they warned me about copyright theft. Then they said, "anyway we don't give a shit about that, but those two guys you just sold to, do you know them?" I said I'd never seen them before, and they said "they are the two biggest drug dealers in London." They thought I'd been selling drugs! They even looked inside the couple of tapes I had left to see if there were any drugs.'

David continued to work on the bridge for a couple of summers, using the money to pay for holidays in Greece and Ibiza. 'I made the couple of hundred quid needed for the flight in half an afternoon's work, while my mates worked on construction sites all summer long. I probably owe the late Curtis Mayfield quite a bit of copyright money. But I was sixteen, what did I know? If you could have just seen the *river* of people that flocked to Camden Lock, people went there because it was different and independent and changing week by week, you could buy tapes, sneak into Roy Ayres, have something to eat, to drink, buy clothes, and all of that was rammed together.'

Foodseller Lou Landin also had huge success, again without a stall but this time in the heart of the market. First she tried selling secondhand clothes, but everyone else seemed to be as well, so 'she just thought she'd bake her own bread,' explains her

mother Hanne, who'd worked at the market ten years earlier. 'She did it at night in her tiny kitchen in her tiny council flat and then we'd make sandwiches. Her bread was organic, way before people used the word organic, and we used homemade mayonnaise, organic eggs, cheese and pickle. We had a system; we piled the sandwiches on a tray and then put them in plastic bags and held them in both arms like a Chinese water carrier. Lou would walk around and sell, and everything would go instantly. You would hear a great cry over Camden Lock; "here comes the girl with the good sandwiches!" Management wasn't keen but somehow she got away with it, mainly because all her food went so quickly. She was out there in all weathers and I would worry about her in the cold, except that people are very hungry when it's cold.'

Eventually Lou got a stall, first temporary and then permanent, and was 'fabulously successful, she would make £400 a day on sandwiches, bread and homemade carrot cake, tea and coffee. For her it was a good money maker, the market was throbbing with people and they swallowed up whatever we took, cake, lassi, they woofed it down.' But Lou realized she couldn't keep baking at home: 'people were beginning to complain

about the noise at night, things being put in and out of the oven, and great big trays being moved around.' So with her stall profits she bought a shop in Chalk Farm, with a proper kitchen, which she ran for the next seven years.

'A lot of business was female-run at Camden Market,' remembers Eric. 'It was very unusual at the time for a woman to be in charge and to set up on her own.' Another successful food seller was Binh Doan who'd arrived in England from Vietnam in 1980. 'I was twenty-four and on my own on a boat. I lived in Camden and I worked as a cashier at a supermarket and did cleaning jobs for rich people in Hampstead. I didn't speak English but I really wanted to work.' First she tried to get a stall at the Lock selling Vietnamese and Chinese souvenirs. 'I saw all the people looking for food and someone asked, "can you cook?" I said "yes." But they wouldn't give me a stall. So I cooked, I put it in a basket and I got on my bike and I sold Vietnamese food, like spring rolls, beef with lemon grass, chicken curry. I made it into lunchboxes. People liked it. They would ask others, "where did you get that from?" "Binh", they said. I started selling to ten to fifteen people, then I was selling to 100 people. I cooked for months.'

But then she was told she couldn't sell food without a licence. 'I went to the Town Hall. I cried for three days. I said "please, I'm a Vietnamese refugee, I don't have much money. I love cooking…"' A stallholder started a petition and gathered 300 signatures, and Binh took it to the Town Hall. 'Hygiene came and inspected my flat where I made the food. I begged Eric and Alan and in the end I got a stall. No one was selling Vietnamese food, only me. It was hard but I was patient.'

Another food outlet in the period was Pratts Restaurant in the West Yard, run by Eric and Annie Foster-Firth. Cathy Palmer remembers: 'Food presented on plates covered with large silver lids would be placed in front of each member of the party and then the lids lifted all at once. Very impressive, but small portions and pretty expensive.'

The Lock offered plenty of ways for people to make a living in the 1980s and provided an outlet for unusual goods. Traders remember a man called Norman who sold Etruscan statues, and one memorable lunchtime he had ten grand in his pocket. But it was for fashion that Camden Market would really become renowned.

7. Fashion in the 1980s

Many would-be designers found Camden an ideal place to start out in the early 1980s, especially now that another market had opened on the High Street. This was Buck Street Market, next to the Electric Ballroom, a famed music venue, and close to the tube station. When nineteen-year-old Wayne Hemingway heard the news, he thought it might help him out of his financial difficulties. He'd been coming to London from Lancashire as a punk from the age of fifteen. 'Camden Lock was always on my route, I was looking for secondhand clothes and not many places were selling them then. There were also a lot of charity shops in Camden. I read in *Time Out* that a new bit of the market was opening, it was cheaper than at the Lock and closer to the tube, so we would be more visible, and people would pass us on their way to the Lock.'

Wayne and his partner Gerardine urgently needed £18 to pay the next week's rent on their flat. 'It was needs must. The cost of a stall was only £6 and we knew the clothes we had to sell would make more than that. We were confident we could sell them because we were pretty cool kids. But we had no plans for the future.' So they turned up on a Saturday morning, were given a stall a few pitches back from the front, and by the end of the day they had made £180. 'We were emphatically successful, we saw we could make money, and we could get the stock. There weren't people out there looking for vintage clothes and we had the eye.' The couple went to 'shoddy yards', still operating near Dewsbury, to buy clothes. 'They were ridiculously cheap, you could get a nice big hessian sack of cotton 50s dresses, and one dress alone could sell for £40.'

Theft was sometimes a problem – 'people would snip the money pouch off your waist and dash with it to the tube station, but Gerardine would chase them' – and, as at the Lock, there were disputes with management and complaints about getting kicked to the worst spot. But for Wayne and Gerardine, who ended up with sixteen permanent stalls, it was the start of a glittering career. Within eighteen months they were making £10,000 every weekend, and also had a temporary stall at the Lock. 'At Camden Market I learnt the history of fashion and the art of design,' says Wayne. 'We were buying clothes from the 1920s to the 70s and in every style there was. We learnt what sells and we learnt about shapes. If there was a rockabilly revival then we got it right, if there was a mod thing going on, we had everything at our fingertips.'

'We were pretty cool kids': Wayne and Gerardine Hemingway at the start of a glittering career

They started selling shoes such as old Dr Martens, the more battered the better, and formed their own label Red or Dead, which won the British Fashion Council's first Street Style Designer of the Year Award. At first their customers were students, but the fame of Camden in the 1980s spread and London was becoming a major fashion capital. Their clients soon included Jean Paul Gaultier, the French haute couture fashion designer, and pop stars of the time such as Marc Almond from the band Soft Cell.

'Camden became a centre for alternative fashion around 1980; this was "post punk", because punk had been the King's Road,' explains Wayne. 'Camden was the "Hard Times" clubby look and then a few years later the London focus for acid house fashion, like Wallabee shoes and smiley face t-shirts. Anyone who went to the dance culture clubs at the turn of the 80s, like Le Beat Route and the Wag Club, places playing rare groove and New York-style post disco disco if you like, also went to Camden.

'Camden was where you got the look': Wayne at his Buck Street stall
Right Wayne and fellow members of the band Diversen, on the banks of the Regent's Canal in Camden

Beat-up Levi 501s and Dr Martens was a very Camden look. Everyone who was cool, like Boy George and Spandau Ballet, everyone you saw at the clubs of Soho on a Friday and Saturday night was there at Camden on Sunday. Anyone wanting to get an affordable version of the McLaren and Westwood 'buffalo' style could put it together at Camden; it became the place to go. While the fashion started in the clubs, Camden was where you got the look and put it together. Lots of international designers came to see people and buy things and their designs were then influenced by Camden. It was the first stopping off point, along with Kensington Market, and a place for youth culture; soon people all around the world knew about Camden.'

Eventually Wayne and Gerardine left Buck Street, having already opened shops in Camden, Manchester, Soho and Covent Garden. 'Red or Dead was on the catwalks by then, it was a dual life, working in the freezing cold in Camden versus the glamour of London Fashion Week, as well as traveling to Paris and Milan. And we had three kids

by then; it was time to hand the stalls over to someone else. Looking back we were unbelievably lucky, it felt like we were part of London on the rise, and we were.'

Camden Lock was soon known as a place to source trendy clothes. Dempsey Dunkley-Clark, who'd started out in 1975, remembers bumping into John Krivine, founder of legendary boutique BOY on the King's Road, and he started buying women's plastic boots from her stall at the Lock. The BOY mail-order catalogue for 1980 included bondage trousers, zip shirts, anarchy shirts, maids' dresses, fluorescent socks, bloodstained t-shirts ('Looks like you've been shot') and Dempsey's £7.90 black booties. She remembers one day 'this guy, a business type, came and bought some long johns with braces and he was trying to impress me with showing me cheque stubs from Tina Turner and I thought, who cares? But it turned out he had a shop on Melrose Avenue in LA. He ignored my rudeness and became my very best customer.' The man was French entrepreneur Michel Perey, and Dempsey began shipping over clothing from other designers, including Patrick Cox

'Everyone you saw at the clubs of Soho on a Friday or Saturday night was there at Camden on Sunday': market regulars Boy George and Marilyn

Far right, The BOY mail-order catalogue for 1980. The King's Road shop sourced women's plastic boots from Lock stallholder Dempsey. The image top right features a teenage Sadie Frost (middle, seated)

Eine Kleine

TROPIC OF **winter'85** FUR AND VELVET
STAND N° 2·40 THE EXHIBITIONISTS BRITISH DESIGN SHOW **olympia**

DEMPSEY DUNKLEY-CLARK 110 SOUTHGATE ROAD LONDON N1 TEL 01-249 3332

Eine Kleine

Far left Models wearing Dempsey's designs, including her trademark leggings
Left Dempsey's business Eine Kleine was praised for being fun, young and funky
Above Stallholder Dempsey with her daughter Alice

and Fred Bare. Things soon became hectic: 'When you're on a stall it's full on, you're there, in the moment, you need to sell things, and people are coming at you constantly, it's front line retail.' She then started her own business, Eine Kleine, praised in the trade press for being fun, young and funky. 'The clue to Eine Kleine's success lies in accessibly-priced layers of cotton velveteen,' explained *Woman'sWearResources*, 'cotton cord panne velvet and fake fur in brights like black, white, yellow, blue and red. Matching accessories complete the look – leggings, hats and mufflers!' Dempsey became renowned as the woman who invented leggings. 'I noticed women at Camden Lock wearing thick tights and ankle warmers; people were very stylish. I wanted something more substantial than tights and not as constricting as jeans.' So she stitched up the fly on army surplus cotton long johns, and dyed them various colours. She then worked out a pattern and had leggings made up, taking the term from a 1930s children's book.

Fashion designer Helen David also found Camden the 'best place to start'. She began at a stall at the Lock around 1982. 'I had no money, I'd just left art college, and I turned up on a Saturday morning and queued. It was quite busy; there were about twenty people after a few stalls and some didn't get one at all. We made hand-printed clothes, it was Hobo fashion, just after the New Romantics, and we printed them during the week, sewed them on a Thursday and Friday, and sold them at the weekend.' She then had a permanent stall, and founded the fashion label English Eccentrics with her sister Judy Purbeck and friend Claire Angel, specialising in hand-printed and hand-embroidered eveningwear and scarves. Helen remembers Camden as 'a mix of cool Londoners and a few tourists. A lot of arty people came by, actors and so on.' When she was offered a shop on the King's Road a couple of years later she left, 'but Camden was a very important launch pad for us.' And what did she learn from her time there? 'To wear big boots! It was really cold in February and the cold crept up your legs. Also I learnt to interact with the public, to discover what people liked and why. I was not a great salesperson, I found it difficult to sell my own things because I was personally attached to what I'd made; it was easier when other people sold it for me. I'm grateful to the market; I had no contacts, no money, no job, there were very few opportunities for young people. There was a real camaraderie, and you always got good advice on footwear!'

In the mid 1980s, Northside hired a PR company to promote the market internationally, and its array of fashion attracted plenty of publicity. *The Chicago Tribune* ran a lengthy piece, describing the Lock as 'a colorful, labyrinthine sprawl of warehouses and tented stalls which cheerfully dispenses everything from grilled hamburgers to handknit sweaters in a festive, casbah-like atmosphere'. Clothing predominated, with stalls entirely devoted to bright socks, wool berets, racks of vintage tweed and wool coats, hand-painted sandals and Edwardian bloomers. 'A basic rule of thumb is if you like it, buy it,' advised the *Tribune*, 'because odds are you won't find your way back to it again.' It stressed that many of London's young fashion and accessories designers had first started on a stall in the market, such as BodyMap, 'whose stretchy, printed sportswear made such a mark on the (American) design scene'.

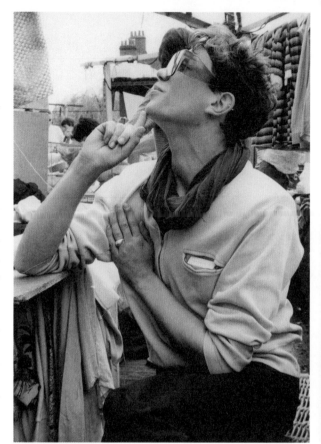

BodyMap, launched by Stevie Stewart and David Holah in 1983, was 'fashion's toast of the mid-Eighties' and drew much of its inspiration from London's thriving clubland scene. The company won numerous design awards and hosted legendary London parties, their outfits were displayed at the Victoria & Albert Museum, and the duo designed costumes for the Michael Clark Dance Company and the Ballet Rambert.

And behind all their success was a single stall at Camden Lock. Stevie had first got the market bug as a fifteen-year-old when she worked at Portobello Road in the 1970s, helping 'two very glamorous sisters who made hippy handmade skirts out of scarves'. By the time she was eighteen, she had her own stall selling accessories, and then she moved to Camden Lock in the late 70s where she made feather earrings. 'I was very entrepreneurial from an early age, I bought the feathers from a woman who sold pheasant skins and guinea fowl wholesale, and I also bought dyed feathers, and the earrings sold in their hundreds.' She soon had a permanent stall, selling punk badges, zipped t-shirts, rubber sandals, and hair accessories. 'I really needed to do a market stall, as I hadn't got a grant to do a degree at Middlesex Polytechnic and the market paid for that, that's where I met David and he began helping out at the weekends.'

'There was quite a hoo-ha setting up the stall,' he remembers, 'putting the tarpaulin up with clips and making it secure, and then taking it all down again. I thought the market was massive then, I never thought it would get any bigger, it had enough already, with food and clothes and everything. Often we would have a check on how much we'd made – we'd ask each other, "have we got a grand yet?" Some days we made a couple of grand, other days just £10, and we'd ask other stallholders if they'd had a good day and compare notes.'

Stevie remembers 'a nice posh guy who sold proper antiques' and the nearby Body Shop stall run by Jenny and Joan, where her mother became manager. 'They sold their cosmetics alongside army surplus, they had a sort of double stall, and as they got bigger they decided to focus on the Body Shop. I spied a hole in the market and bought up their contacts. We bought hundreds of army surplus "dead stock", winceyette pyjamas

that were going to prisons but had never been sent, and we got them dyed. They were collarless tunics and drawstring trousers and we slung beads around them and accessorised them in a sort of Kenzo style.' The pyjamas were sold for £4.95, £7 if you bought both pieces, and Stevie was able to buy a London flat with the profits. Their customers were the 'yummy mummies of the time', explains David, 'trendy people looking for bargains', such as Mariella Frostrup and Annie Lennox.

The duo launched BodyMap after they left college, financed from the proceeds of the market stall, and continued to sell their wares at the Lock. 'The stall wasn't BodyMap, it was Market Map,' says David. 'We used last season's fabrics and remnants from BodyMap to make ra-ra skirts, which were a big seller, and t-shirts. The main BodyMap line went global, but we kept our humble little stall at Camden Lock selling Market Map.'

'We were selling to huge department stores by then,' explains Stevie, 'so obviously we couldn't sell that season's collection on a market stall, so it was a type of diffusion line and it was a huge coup for people to buy these pieces or ends of lines, and we dressed wooden manikins and hung them up over the stall. I worked at the Lock for nearly 20 years, it was a community and people looked out for each other, there were always kids falling in the canal inlet that had to be fished out. We learned first hand about retail experience and how to deal with people.'

In the early 80s club styles were varied, says David, with 'left over punk styles and remnants of the New Romantic era, but the Blitz Kids were ruling. Designers like Stephen Linard and Melissa Caplan were selling their designs to pop starlets, Boy George was

Left The Lock was 'a great way of showing work': Ian Morris modelling some of his printed textiles
Above Stallholders at the Lock, which had become 'London's trendiest Sunday hang-out'

wearing Sue Clowes for the iconic Culture Club look, stylists like Ray Petri and Caroline Baker were influencing looks on the streets, and individual street fashions were shown in i-D and *The Face*; it was all about individualism and experimenting with style.'

As with all outdoor markets, the weather had a big impact on trade. While David remembers the IRA bombs in London in the 1980s, and 'lots of warnings about being aware of suspicious behaviour, word was spread around the market to watch out for…I don't know what really, boxes and packages I suppose, but then there are lots of packages at a market', it was a sudden thunderstorm that always had a more dramatic effect on sales.

In the mid 80s *The Daily Express* dubbed Camden Lock 'London's trendiest Sunday hang-out…many of Britain's top designers started out with stalls here', and countless teenagers made the pilgrimage to Camden Lock on the hunt for fashion. 'I used to come all the way down from Bedfordshire on a Sunday – a round trip of 35 miles – on the National Express coach just to go to Camden Market,' remembers Wendy Jones. 'The ticket cost £3. I was seventeen and I fancied becoming a goth. I'm very pale and I dyed my hair and my eyebrows pitch black: it looked absolutely dreadful; the eyebrows were a particularly bad mistake. I wore a black pinafore dress, a black-fringed shawl that used to belong to my grandmother, black tights, and pearls – all cheap as chips. I wanted to be creative and there was an extreme sense of excitement in Camden. It was worth the coach ride to get there.'

While traders were quick to take advantage of the interest in clothing, some, like Ian Morris, had mixed experiences at Camden Lock. He'd completed a degree in textiles at his hometown of Loughborough, and had moved to London where he worked evenings at a restaurant in Chalk Farm. 'That's where I got the market buzz. It was a great way of showing work, rather than approaching shops. Camden Lock was a creative hub.' After going to the market every Saturday at the crack of dawn he eventually got a permanent stall. Along with a college friend Helen, they managed to get a pitch in the prestigious black shed: 'it was a prime position, and we sold printed textiles which we made at our studio in Wapping. What we sold was unusual, the fact we had printed fashion put us in good stead. But it was competitive, and there was a lot of flirting going on; people would cry "hi Eric!" when they didn't know him at all. And he was as gruff as anything.

'Our customers were quite fashiony people, and shops came and sourced from the market as well. Lots of people had just left art college; there was an explosion of British talent at that point. There was a London look and people were buying into that scene. It was quite a vibrant place; you'd see people wandering around like Marilyn. The problem was that on a slow day I would walk around and spend all the profits.'

Ian used Camden Lock as a stepping-stone to gain a stall at Kensington Market and then dropped Camden, fed up with unloading in the morning and working in miserable weather. However he returned a couple of years later with another colleague, and had a front pitch near the road. 'We were selling the same things, like printed cushions and t-shirts, but being outside for fashion is not great, it was like corridors with people inching past and no room to try on and the loos were disgusting. The whole thing of queuing up in the morning was tedious, and you didn't know where you would be put, you could be stuck in a corner or next to the food stall and by the end of the day all our clothes stank of hamburgers. The weather was awful. The canopy filled with water and when there was a gust of wind you got completely drenched. It was so cold that one day we spent all our profits buying miniatures from the off-licence. I sound like a grumpy old bugger, although I was a grumpy young bugger in those days. But the market was a great eye-opener for a young lad hitting the London scene; it had a great deal of kudos to be part of the market. It certainly made you "street wise" spending a little time on a stall.'

Left Dempsey's daughter Daisy would often visit Stevie Stewart's stall to get 'BodyMapped' with make up and accessories
Below Clothing dominated at the Lock in the 80s, with entire stalls devoted to socks, coats, sandals or hats

Joe Swift was also attracted to the Lock as a place to sell clothes. He'd first worked at the market around 1980 when he was fourteen, selling sweatshirts for 'some bloke who used to pick me up in a van at 5am'. It was Joe's presence at the market that had inspired Anna Kusner to try her luck on a stall, which she only gave up when she lost all her profits selling swimming costumes. Joe returned to the market a few years later, sharing a stall with his friend Julie, whose mother Janet had decided market life wasn't for her a few years earlier. 'I'd been travelling and brought back some batik jackets from Bali,' explains Joe. 'Then I became a bit of a yuppie, got a bank loan and went on some government scheme, and went back to Bali and had clothes made up. Julie is quite a "hassly" person, she gave Eric such a hard time that we always got a stall; eventually we had a great double permanent stall. I felt sorry for Eric, he had a pressured job and people were always harassing him.

'Opposite us was a couple selling hats – panamas and flat caps – and they did a roaring trade. There was also a man selling strange punky clothes and he would go to the off-licence and bring back bottles in brown paper bags. There were people selling similar stuff to us, but no one trod on our toes, there were no major ructions and we got on with everyone. There was one old bloke and his wife who sold Victorian bath taps. He would lay out four double taps, all lovely polished brass, and put them on a nice bit of black cloth and sell them. Then they packed up and went. They did this every Saturday; sometimes they had left by 11am, the lucky beggars.'

Joe and Julie then moved into an office and storage space above a shop opposite the market, where their company Bagus sold wholesale to shops including Harrods, and made waistcoats for Soul II Soul, the chart-topping local band known for their Funki Dred clothing.

'I remember Camden Market very fondly,' says Joe. 'That's because deep down I think I'm a secondhand car salesman. I enjoyed telling someone they looked great in a jacket. I enjoyed bartering. And it was a trendy place to be, Camden Lock was *the* place to go at the weekend.'

Yet while the Lock now attracted thousand of visitors, not everyone was happy with the way Camden Town was changing, and they were even unhappier when the tourists began to arrive. Until the late 80s the Lock was 'an interesting social experiment', says Eric Reynolds; 'then it became something different, and that's when the tourists began.'

8. The Tourists Arrive

There's a great crowd of tourists and they're coming down the street
Pleased as punch with brand new Doctor Martens on their feet
From 'Camden Town', Suggs, 1995

Overseas visitors first began making a beeline to Camden Lock in the late 1980s when Camden Town had a reputation as a busy, bohemian place. 'From its origins as one of London's poorest quarters, Camden has blossomed as one of its liveliest,' declared one newspaper. 'The market at the pretty Lock started the gentrification process.' While there were still plenty of handcrafted goods on sale, residents complained the area was growing more like Carnaby Street every day, becoming 'tacky and packed with tourists'. There were mixed feelings about the Lock's success. It was accused of being artificial and trendy, and there were fears that tourists would 'take over' Camden Town, crowding pavements and buses, leaving litter at the canalside, and forcing out local shops to make way for boutiques. 'At the end of the day it was really unpleasant,' remembers Eric Reynolds. 'We made a success of Sunday trading but we were ankle deep in rubbish. We had our own cleaners at the Lock, but on the high street it was everywhere and it took a while before the council took action.' Craftspeople, meanwhile, complained rents were about to treble; units had become retail shops rather than the original workshops, and they were opposed to the continuing plans for development.

One of the big draws for tourists was that Camden Lock had become a magnet for punks, first attracted to the area in the mid 70s. By the late 80s, the place was 'kohl-black with punks', reported *The Observer*, and Camden also became known for the ease with which people could buy drugs. 'In the early days there were two people who sold paraphernalia,' says Eric, 'funny little pipes that they would sell along with instruments and other things and I don't think I knew what it was really.' But by the late 80s visitors remember stalls selling pipes, bongs, hubbly-bubblies, rolling mats and machines, and cigarette papers in all sorts of colours and patterns. As yet, however, drugs were not seen as a major problem.

Camden Lock became a magnet for punks, first attracted to the area in the mid 70s

Young entrepreneurs continued to compete for a pitch at the market, taking advantage of the influx of tourists. Marice Cumber, who'd first discovered the market as a teenager in the mid 70s, now started selling hand-painted ceramics. 'We had some really great days,' she remembers. 'There were lots of Japanese and Americans tourists and I could sell out at Christmas. Eric wrote names on strips of paper and then fanned them out and picked a name. He was lord of the manor and we were desperate young people. If you were lucky, your name was picked and eventually we got a permanent stall.' She remembers a man called Hilton who sold hot cider: 'it was just apple juice that he heated up and sold to tourists, he was like the guy from *The Singing Detective*, very angry but with a heart of gold', a man known as 'Goblin Boy' who sold models of imps and hobbits, and a man called Mark who sold 'secondhand faux antiques; we called him "big Mark up" because he made a killing and we resented that'.

Like many stallholders, Marice made firm friends at the market. 'There was a real cross section, from hardened market people to arts graduates and people who imported things from India. It was a real learning curve, stalls were around £30 a day, and you could get nothing when it rained, but people were supportive and minded your stall. It was a community of arts graduates and there was an opportunity that you don't have anymore. We made money out of creativity. One man made jewellery and cuff links out of piano keys, and I remember Jean Paul Gaultier coming around, looking for talent.'

Above A flower stall at Camden Market
Right 'We made money out of creativity': (top right) a pottery unit in the West Yard; (bottom right) a craftsperson at work

Marice, along with her boyfriend, set up Mac Products, which sold to department stores such as John Lewis and Liberty, and eventually they bought their own studio. 'Camden Lock was an interesting journey,' she says. 'It was a stepping-stone in life; working on a stall is hard graft and you learn a lot. You learn about rejection when you don't sell and that prepares you, you learn selling skills and communication skills. I don't regret one minute.'

Such was the influx of overseas visitors that one young trader Kee, who worked on a flower stall, remembers 'tourists asking to take pictures of me because they thought I was a traditional London flower girl!' But not everyone benefited from the tourists. Ian Morris, who first started at the market in the early 80s, returned for the third time with his business partner Cath. 'We started making printed ceramics and it was a complete disaster. In the late 80s, no one was interested; Europeans didn't want plates and mugs. Sometimes we didn't get a stall, it was so popular, a lot were permanent and very few were vacant. The market didn't have a great reputation any more, there was not the same kudos as there

had been in the early 80s, it was losing its cool.' So instead they started selling contemporary china and glassware to shops such as Bergdorf Goodman and Conran.

But teens still flocked to the Lock for casual jobs, like Claire who worked on a secondhand Levi stall. She'd first come to the Lock as a child. 'Dingwalls was where I played out with my cousins while my auntie hung out and listened to music, there were just a handful of stalls and it was quite fleamarkety on a Sunday.' But now she was a teenager: 'I used to go out all night raving then do a shift at the market all day long. I'd dance all night, have a cup of tea, and stand there all day, then go out all night again. I had a lot of energy in my twenties. It was sociable, everyone was doing it, and it was cash in hand. You didn't have to commit, I could just say I'd be back the next weekend, and we got paid £20-30 a day.'

At the end of the 1980s, with Northside's lease about to expire, the company came up with a £10 million expansion plan, initially a joint development with UK Land Limited. Northside produced an advert 'Camden Lock is Building up' which promised, 'More of a good thing can be even better.' It showed a top-hatted Victorian gentleman consulting plans, side by side with a hard-hatted modern-day worker. The advert announced they were in the process of building shops, a new pub, a courtyard market – all to be open every day – and a new market yard. 'Visit us now,' it implored, 'midweek when it is peaceful, or at weekends when it's not.'

Northside also produced a video, which opened with the words, 'At 8.30 on any Sunday morning, when most of London is fast asleep, there is one place where things are stirring…by breakfast the regulars are set up and those who don't hire a permanent spot are being allocated a position.' The video showed scenes of June's food stall, Le Routier, and the Body Shop, as well as musicians, a unicyclist, and

jugglers performing on the canalside. 'It's a melting pot,' said one customer admiringly; 'it doesn't matter what colour you are, what age you are, whether you're poor...' The video emphasised the busyness of the Lock, with friendly traders offering unique things in an alternative place full of 'vigorous' commercial activity. 'If anyone goes to London,' explained Eric Reynolds, 'they will go to the Tower, they will go to the Palace, and they will go here.'

The new development included 40,000 square feet of space in part of the site fronting Chalk Farm Road, with a pedestrian entrance from the main road leading to a yard with shops on one side. There would also be a new canalside pub, with open terraces and stairs down to the yard. But the biggest plan was for a 'Victorian style retail hall, which will take part of the market indoors for the first time', with studio workshops above, as well as penthouse studios and offices. 'Peter and Bill didn't want people to be able to tell what was old and what was new,' explains architect John Dickinson, 'and on Chalk Farm Road they wanted two levels of shops. The design was closely modelled on existing

Left Eric Reynolds (centre) with a team of market managers including Alan Jones (top far left)
Above Models built for Northside's £10-million expansion plan, which included a new Victorian-style retail hall fronting Chalk Farm Road

canal buildings, in particular a canalside site at the north end of Ladbroke Grove, which had ramps and elevation details which I incorporated into the four-storey buildings. The case officers were so helpful, and we had built two scale models, so planning permission was obtained first time round for this latest scheme.' The Ladbroke Grove building was Portobello Dock, where Peter, Bill and John had drawn up a scheme to 'do another Camden Lock' in West London, which was then presented to Kensington Council. 'Unfortunately,' says Peter, 'we were seen off by bigger fish in the form of the Virgin Group who took it over for their offices.'

Having designed the structures fronting Chalk Farm Road, 'the remaining space between Dingwalls and the new buildings would have been rather overshadowed,' remembers John, 'and so I decided to cover it with glass, creating the Retail Hall.' The brick and cast iron structure was built on the site of the original 70s market and based on a Victorian gas showroom, now part of the Birmingham Museum and Art Gallery. 'I was

Above The iconic sign on Chalk Farm Bridge, painted 'to promote the fact this is Camden Lock on the North London line'
Right Artist John Bulley at work, as featured in *The Ham & High*

reading *The Architects' Journal* about the refurbishment at the gas hall in Birmingham,' remembers John, 'and I looked at the photo and it looked stunning. I showed it to Peter and Bill and we got the train to Birmingham and they let us have a look around. The layout looked good; I wanted a glass roof flooded with daylight and a gallery, and it gave us a clue of how to design it.'

The new development created a further 20,000 square feet of studio and shop space, as well as a refurbished Dingwalls and a new comedy club, Jongleurs in the East Yard. But some of those at the Lock worried that the best days were over, at a time when the yuppie mantra was that greed is good. 'When people started to be there for the profit it changed,' says food seller June Carroll; 'it wasn't reward for hard work, it was just greediness.' Until the early 80s, visitors were mainly local Londoners, but as the Lock

became known worldwide, products changed and handmade items began to be replaced with imported goods.

'It was less about fun and more about shifting units,' says bookseller Chris Overfield. 'People used to sponsor their travels at the market, then the new kids on the block went to East End storehouses. When we started, tourists came in coach loads at 7am chasing bric-à-brac, Japanese and Americans bought books and it was heaven. Then the antiquey people fell off, there was nothing quirky and the tourists just came to see and be seen.'

'People were lovely in the early days,' says Eric Reynolds. 'They went to Peru and bought things back, but they were replaced by people who went to the Cash and Carry. And by then we had other markets around us, such as the Stables next door, they contributed to our success, because it increased the general critical mass, but the other markets weren't as selective, there were huge numbers of people selling t-shirts and knock off this, that and the other. People came out of Camden Town tube and it was wall-to-wall market.'

It was now that Northside was finally given permission to paint the iconic sign 'Camden Lock' on Chalk Farm Bridge. Several years earlier, British Rail had been doing remedial work and when Northside heard that they weren't intending to put back the hoardings, Peter Wheeler wrote to ask 'if a joint sign of some benefit and style could be put up on the bridge to promote the fact that this is Camden Lock on the North London line'. Permission was eventually granted, as long as they arranged the artwork and erection themselves.

In 1989 Northside hired mural artist and sign writer John Bulley and a team of shop painters and artists. 'I thought it would be a laugh to make it look like a couple of blokes were painting the lettering whilst hanging precariously off the lip of the bridge,' explains Bulley on his website. 'I came across a newspaper article the other day which described the painting as an icon but made no mention of the artist. I'm not having that, I thought, it's about time I was given credit for inadvertently creating a London landmark!' The press reported that the workers depicted on the bridge were based on two of Bulley's colleagues, while others believe Bulley portrayed himself, looking over his shoulder at the road below.

With the bridge sign in place, it was time for some major development work and this, the second major phase in the story of Camden Lock, led to significant upheaval. 'There was a fear the place would die when the three year development plan started,' remembers office manager Cathy Palmer. 'We had to rail off places and temporarily cover the wharf so we could move stalls back and keep the market going, but it survived.' Northside phased the development, hiring an old canal boat and floating it into the wharf and taking the plug out to sink it. Eric then built over the boat with scaffolding and timber boarding, reducing the width of the basin just enough for the Waterbus, and then put the stallholders on top. 'It was a lot of work keeping the market open,' explains Alan Jones. 'They could have saved millions and done it in half the time if they'd closed it but it would have lost its vibrancy. It's not a shopping centre, there is the human element to a market and that is the strength of the site.'

According to Northside, the idea behind the development was to return to the early traditions of the market as a centre for craft workers, with traders in the Market Hall and workshops offering products 'created and sold by local artists and designers as well as quality imported items'. When the hall opened in the summer of 1991, *The Evening Standard* gave the Lock an award, declaring it was 'a credit to London'. Town planner Richard Humphreys remembers plenty of arguments with Camden Council over the redevelopment of the East Yard, 'but John told me that when it opened, someone from the council's planning department made a visit on other business and enquired whether it was a listed building. And John said, "no it's brand new!"

Craftspeople were now offered twenty-year leases rather than three, but rents once again increased, and the new development was not without bitter controversy. Journalist Simon Regan made a series of attacks in an article called 'The Jigsaw of Camden Lock' in *Scallywag*, a now defunct magazine that was no stranger to libel threats, accusing Northside of driving out leaseholders and stallholders. He cited the case of one trader

Below The Lock was declared 'a credit to London' by the *Evening Standard*
Right Market life continued throughout the three-year expansion
Bottom right An image from the back of *Scallywag Magazine*

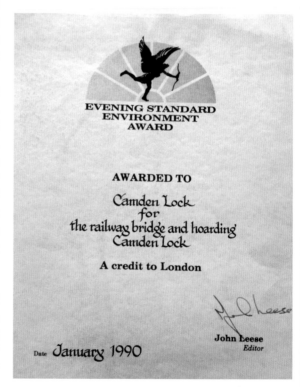

EVENING STANDARD ENVIRONMENT AWARD

AWARDED TO

Camden Lock
for
the railway bridge and hoarding
Camden Lock

A credit to London

Date January 1990

John Leese
Editor

who'd taken the company to court, alleging that large vans had been 'ordered to park in front of (his) shop', a visiting fair had been 'encouraged to park a generator nearby' and acid parties were going on nearby. The *Scallywag* insisted that the Lock had fallen 'into purely commercial hands', the original aim of a Crafts Centre had been 'gradually buried', and instead it was a 'hotbed of commercial intrigue'. Eric recalls a couple of court cases in the early 90s, 'People wanted to hold the development to ransom, it happens when there is change. But there was no worse conflict than at any other time.'

Indeed Cathy Palmer, who had to chase tenants for rent, recalls 'I once heard a tenant say that Camden Lock was the only place she knew of where the landlord sent out their reminders with 'love' above the signature; it wasn't all conflict! Not all rent reminders went out with love, but there were

The Heart of London

a few I was fond of, they were very nice people.'

However it was at this point that some craftspeople moved out. 'I could see the writing on the wall,' says glass specialist Marc Gerstein who'd had a stall the day the market first started. 'As soon as you're successful a landlord increases your rent until you're not successful, that's universal, it's not just Camden Market. I didn't like paying rent, who does? I needed to buy bigger quantities of glass and I needed more space.'

Marc had been at the Lock for nearly eighteen years, but in 1992 he bought a derelict building in Chalk Farm and left. 'I tried to still keep a stall,' he says, 'but the market had changed, people were coming for fashion, which wasn't what I was selling.'

Accusations of commercialism at the Lock continued – the products on sale were more likely to be imported than handmade, unlicensed stallholders were selling sweat tops and t-shirts along Camden High Street, residents complained of congestion and litter and feared the market was draining the

Many of the well-known faces at the market had wandered over from the nearby MTV studios, originally the headquarters of TV-am and known for the large plastic eggcups on its roof

area of useful shops. Overcrowding was also a problem and the Lock was so packed that passengers at Camden Tube Station weren't allowed to get off at the station at weekends.

The *Daily Express* described 'stalls selling flower-child frocks and PVC underwear… tourists standing shoulder to shoulder at weekends since they discovered the market… this is Camden, and you could love to hate it.' It also identified the 'Camdenite'. 'They will wear grunge, Doc Martens or clogs…they are often expensively squalid and can be writers and actors who prefer the debauchery of Camden to the obvious trendiness of Notting Hill.'

There were now 10 million visitors a year to the various Camden markets, with an estimated turnover of over £50 million. In a questionnaire distributed to stallholders in 1992, traders were asked whether they had any celebrity customers. 'Yes, many,' wrote one, 'but we respect their privacy.' Others were more forthcoming: 'a lot of the directors at Channel 4', said one stallholder; 'pop stars and dancers' said another. Stella, a clothing stall, named Giorgio Armani and Andy MacDowell among their customers, while clothing unit Scarecrow listed Meg Mathews, Helena Christensen, David Bowie, Bill Wyman, Sinead O'Connor, and Steve Tyler. Abbey Bookshop added Ben Elton, Jools Holland, Will Self and Deborah Moggach.

Other stallholders remember pop star Adam Ant, *Baywatch* actor David Hasselhoff, who 'walked around with a gaggle of girls', Gloria Estefan and Melinda Messenger. Many of the well-known faces had wandered over from the nearby MTV studios, part of a canalside complex designed in 1981. This had initially been the headquarters of TV-am, Britain's first commercial breakfast TV station, designed by Terry Farrell, and known for the distinctive large plastic eggcups on its roof. Then in 1993 MTV, the first TV channel solely devoted to music, took over the building, setting up shop in an area well known for its local music scene, for its scores of young people, and for its independent record labels and record shops.

Most stallholders at Camden Lock said they had had plenty of media interest – from newspapers, magazines, TV and radio – but one said the Lock was no longer vibrant: 'it's not current, and there is no wow factor, it's stuck in hippy laid back image.' Many wanted more promotion, and better weekday trade.

Bookseller Chris Overfield said the idea of a craft market had been a joke for years as 'the chaotic efforts of a bunch of hopeless hippies was exploited by the children of Thatcher's era and now needs to redefine itself and find a soul.' Another stallholder complained that 'we see far less of the affluent middle-class, middle-aged customer.... It's all Italians and Japanese in their twenties.' But traders were still desperate for a stall and Northside's archives are full of begging letters to Eric Reynolds. When one company applied for 'an American sports-day concept site', the scrawled response was 'not our style!'

There were now around 400 stalls, open from 9am to 7pm at the weekend, and in a lengthy *Time Out* spread, the market was named as the city's fourth biggest tourist attraction and 'the nearest thing London has to a Bohemian quarter....Camden Market has, depending on your viewpoint, blossomed or spread, cancer-like, to three main areas.' Some traders didn't bother applying for a stall, but fly-pitched on the canal towpath. 'Every now and again I had to pick up all the gear and run,' remembers one such trader. 'There was a man who had smiley face acid t-shirts and he would pull up with the van, open the back and sell everything. We sold 10,000 t-shirts in six months. There were a lot of escape routes at Camden, especially around the Stables, it was like a warren. We had lookouts and when the police came you could quickly disappear, or you could have a car waiting and bang, that was it. Lots of people were doing it. Every couple of weeks the police came and lots of people were cautioned, but the police saw it as a joke; they had no idea how much money we made.' He recalls 'knock off perfume boys', someone selling 'a little bit of basil on the bridge' and those trying to pass off dodgy £20 notes.

But although Camden Lock was now a weekday market, inside the Market Hall trade was sluggish to begin with. 'Someone had the idea of doing a themed market,' says Alan, 'but what we did was develop cooperatives. We said to traders, "why don't you run your own group of stalls on a cooperative basis, get a group of ten traders on the same aisle, and run it all week, instead of taking stock home and bringing it back again?" We also gave them a discount. They were all there at the weekends, but in the week they took turns and that worked, it encouraged people to trade seven days a week and increased the number of customers and there was a sense that people were helping each other. The relationship between stallholders is very strong. Camden has developed on an almost club atmosphere with a real sense of belonging.'

However, some traders from the 80s left in the early 90s, such as food seller Jacey Sallés. 'There was more food, and business suffered; before that

Stall of Fame

From a standing start in 1974, Camden Lock has become the largest street market in Europe. One of its founders, the urbane Eric Reynolds, has now spread his wings to develop Spitalfields, in the heart of Jack the Ripper's East End. Can he repeat the Camden phenomenon? ASHLEY NIELD hears his pitch

Above Eric Reynolds featured in many magazine spreads
Right A map of the Lock and area from the early 1990s

we were the only place to come. But I learnt the tools of the trade to open my own business.' Jacey and co-worker Chris Demetriou opened Café Mania on Greek Street, which they ran for six years. 'June Carroll's biggest influence was her mantra that "people eat with their eyes first darling" and the food always had to be beautifully presented and colour coordinated.'

Other long-term traders stayed at the Lock, but moved pitches several times over the years. Bookseller Chris had a double stall in the West Yard in the early 90s: 'No one wanted to be in the West Yard but it was the making of us. At 5am we unloaded a ton of books, it took two hours to set the stall up and we didn't go home until 9pm, how we did

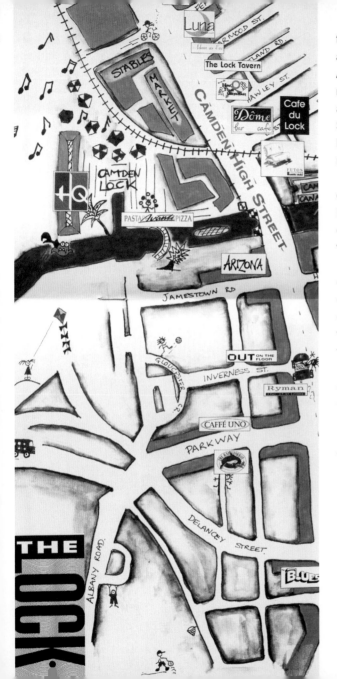

that for years I don't know. Then we were asked if we wanted a shop and the idea of locking a door and going home was like, yes please!' At one point Chris opened an art bookshop. 'I never lost as much money in my life. It was pure arrogance, everyone said I was mad and that was like a red rag to a bull. It was an unmitigated disaster. Students couldn't afford to spend £20 on art books and people who have them and can afford them don't want to sell them. Within a month I realised it was a total disaster.'

Leatherworker David Bristow also moved in the early 90s, to a downstairs shop. He was still experimenting with designs, such as his famed 'belt with measles' which 'hung in the shop for months and eventually an Italian tried to haggle for it and I said "no", because he was quite rude. Then he came back and offered the right price and I said "no". Everyone said I was mad, but someone else bought it a couple of weeks later.' David also made a belt for Nicko McBrain, the drummer with Iron Maiden. 'He came in one day and said "can you do something with a couple of dragons on it?" Someone told me he wore it in a video, but he's the drummer so he was sitting down and you couldn't see it. But I was very proud of that belt.'

Other traders actually returned to the Lock in the 90s, such as designer Dempsey Dunkley-Clark, who'd left in the late 80s. She opened a shop called Archangel in the 'beautiful, elegant Market Hall', selling candles and incense. 'I thought, do I want to do this again? I'd lost all interest in fashion, but Eric said, "just have it for a year," and I stayed for the next fifteen years!'

9. Traders in the 1990s

By the mid 90s the market was thriving again. Camden had been designated the epicentre of Britpop, bands like Blur, Oasis and Pulp had strong links to the area, and tourists came to scour the Lock for fashion. One stallholder sold army surplus clothing, her bestselling item being German army t-shirts; others sold African shirts, 1950s bikers' jackets, afghan coats, 60s print dresses, flares and platforms from the 70s. There was also more of an array of food, with Indonesian, English and Italian cuisine, while hair braiders on the bridge charged £5 a go. According to one press report, goods on sale also included a human skull. The Lock still hosted events, with theatre shows and Zulu warriors, and two foodsellers, a Spanish man and Italian woman, held their wedding reception in the West Yard just as Peter and Kay Wheeler had done some twenty years earlier.

Many traders in the mid 90s still used their profits to travel, bringing back clothing and jewellery from Asia. Claire, who first worked at the market in the late 80s, returned in the mid 90s after a couple of years travelling. Along with her partner Tony Winter she invested money and bought stock for a stall. 'We bought a type of material produced in the northeast of Thailand; it was a very poor area that wasn't good for farming, and it was an alternative income there. I didn't like the idea of buying cheap t-shirts and selling them at inflated prices so I found a supplier and I worked with this lady, and chose the colours I wanted. We had cargo and drawstring trousers and spaghetti dresses, we used her designs and I made my own as well.

'I knew I could rock up to Camden and get a casual plot. We worked on the stall for a few months, made our money and left. We started in April and by July we were done. There were a lot of people who travelled in winter and did the market in summer and at the end of the day we all went to the Stag's Head pub. A woman next to us sold real linen from China, mine looked more like hemp, but we did brilliantly next to each other. We had a double stall in the West Yard and so did she and customers would buy off both of us, although hers was more expensive. It was hard work setting up. Men's clothes went easily, but with the women's I used to change several times a day to show people what there was. When it was sunny it went really well, on rainy days I just got a blanket out and slept on the boxes of stock, because you had to go there to keep the pitch.'

The 90s band Nervous included several market managers: Keith Holden centre (his father Bernie behind him), Dickie Cripps to his left and Justin Travis to his right

'What we sold was breezy, hippy traveller wear,' explains Tony. 'I didn't actually wear it myself, I'm not that sort of person, but people found it nostalgic. We could see a hole in the market, lots of people travelled to Thailand and there were a lot of tourists from sunny climes. People would say, "cool, I saw those trousers in Thailand; oh they're £10? In Thailand they're £2" and I'd say, "well you go get them then!" Some days we made £150, others £900. Everybody knew everybody. Alan and the other managers would pick and choose whom they wanted; they didn't want some tosh from China.' He remembers famous faces such as Noel Gallagher, who 'cruised through wearing a big sheepskin coat and massive sunglasses', as well as Kate Moss, and nights spent at the club HQ with DJ Paul 'Trouble' Anderson.

Another traveller was Donovan. 'I went travelling around Asia and I was sending back gear to my mum, she had a roomful of stuff, clothes and statues and bamboo and she was freaking out so I ended up going to Camden Market. Someone had a stall and they sold my stuff and we split it 50/50. I sold everything, and went straight back to Asia!' He then returned and ran a stall for six years, selling jewellery from Bali, India and Thailand in the Market Hall during the week, some of which he designed himself, and outside at the weekend. 'It was a good and easy business. I could sell sand to Arabs; I could do the chat. You'd ask someone to look after your stall, visit each other, we all knew each other from Thailand, we'd go off to buy, to Africa, to South America, and then come back. At the end of April we all met at Camden. It was a proper little family. You would see people in Thailand, then at Camden, and then at a festival like Womad. We would wish people the best of luck.' He remembers, market managers would 'put you right next to another jewellery stall and if you gave them any lip they would make you wait right to the end before giving you a stall, people got the hump, it was their livelihood.' He also remembers occasional outbursts, with one staff member being 'punched in the face when he asked for rent', and another being hit with a bottle. There were also disputes between stallholders. 'There were fights, such as if someone blocked the walkway between your stall, or if they'd gone to the same place and got the same gear. One man did very well selling bum bags, two weeks later someone else had been to Nepal and came back with exactly the same stuff; they went to the pub and had a fight. Another time someone smacked another trader in the face and threw him in the canal. One day a man was buying some jewellery from me and he said another stallholder had told him my stuff wasn't silver and it kicked off, there was a bit of animosity. They'd said it about other traders as well and at the end of the day when they came to load their van they found the tyres slashed.'

It was at the Lock that Donovan says he learned how to hustle. 'I already knew that but at Camden I took it to a new level. And I learned never to take people at face value, so many people selling had other things going on, they were artists and musicians and writers and the market funded that. One couple were putting their money into making alternative energy sources.'

But business could still be tough. Stallholder Janice Issitt started work at the market in the mid 90s, selling goods in the Market Hall. 'I'd been made redundant from my job in the music business, but I'd always made things and I'd sold old clothes at Portobello. At Camden I handmade pressed flowers between glass, and made them into clocks

Amy Winehouse worked at the Lock as a fifteen-year-old. Above, street graffiti after her death; top right, performing at a Camden music venue; bottom right, at the Hawley Arms.

and jewellery. For the first six months I had a stall outside because all the rest were taken. After Christmas many stallholders took a holiday and I saw that as my chance, I was too frightened before that to ask for one inside, but Alan eventually moved me in. The philosophy was that to be inside you had to be selling things that were handmade.'

But then Janice says other traders began selling goods similar to hers. 'People tried to get stalls close to where you worked selling the same things, which was incredibly cheeky. But there's not much you can do except tell market management, "they're undercutting and they might be getting it made in a foreign country."' And while there was a core of stallholders who helped each other, she also remembers the occasional outburst: 'I was hit by another stallholder, she had a go at me about all sorts of things. I told her she was talking rubbish and she slapped me round the face! She was jealous of the money I was taking.'

On the whole though, stallholders were firm friends. Kee, who started off on the flower stall in the 80s, was now selling Bang on the Door t-shirts and she remembers the 90s as her favourite time. 'It was good fun, even when it was miserable and cold, it was a laugh, people got on well, there was lots of banter, it was a social thing. When it was freezing cold we got scrumpy jack from the Hawley Arms, and we all went to the pub after work.'

She remembers a music stall trader who used to play *Chattanooga choo choo* over and over again, a man who stood in the entrance of the market playing a stringed instrument and singing Beatles songs, and a fifteen-year-old entrepreneur who sold cappuccino. This was Eddie Ramon, a young Israeli whom Maggie French remembers fifteen-year-old Amy Winehouse having a crush on. 'Amy worked on Saturdays at Kate Lahav's clothes stall next to Eddie, and she used to try very hard to get his attention.' A few years later and singer Amy Winehouse would become an award winning household name, frequently performing at Camden's music venues and a regular at the Hawley Arms.

Like many stallholders, Kee returned to the Lock repeatedly over the years. 'Every time I stopped working at the market I thought, thank God I'm never going back, I don't want to stay in this rut. It was tiring and hard work and I wasn't paid very much. But you could always get a job at the Lock and I worked there on and off for fifteen years. I learned to be tolerant working at Camden Market; there were so many people with different needs and demands. It was a very bustling place and I'm quite a quiet person. It taught me about the diversity of things from around the world which I'd had no clue about until then, it gave me the idea to travel, I went to India and Thailand and it created an interest in that.'

The 1990s saw two important legal developments that would affect both Camden Town and the Lock. The first was the Sunday Trading Act in 1994, and then at the end of April 1995, Camden became the first place in England to allow extended drinking hours on a Sunday, in advance of new laws which meant pubs near markets could serve alcohol from midday to 10.30pm. Camden offered a taste of things to come, and people travelled across London for a prolonged Sunday drink, before the new licensing laws came into effect.

And now more change was on the way. Camden Council sold off their old recycling depot at Suffolk Wharf, which had been derelict for years, for £2.5 million, and it was developed into a three-storey complex of restaurants, shops and offices, designed by Piers Gough, behind and around the old lock-keeper's cottage. This included a glass-faced 132-bedroom Holiday Inn hotel, with restaurant and bar along the canal, facing the back of the market. It was named 'The Glass House on the Lock', reflecting the widespread fame of the area.

Things had certainly changed from the days of a filthy waterway surrounded by derelict buildings: now canalside property was in demand and previously empty buildings with pigeon-infested floors were becoming expensive real estate. At the back of the market was a new pathway and a widened quayside, all the better to draw the crowds in across the roving bridge.

All this seemed very strange to the original 1970s stallholders who, on the market's twentieth anniversary in 1994, went back to try their luck. 'I think it was Eric's idea,' remembers silversmith Sarah Jones, 'and it was hopeless. My stuff was too expensive.

Above 'Doing the *Reservoir Dogs* thing': Alan Jones (right) took over from Eric Reynolds, with fellow managers Eamon Stack (centre) and (left) Barny Crockford
Top right On the market's twentieth anniversary some of the original 70s traders came back to try their luck
Bottom Alan Jones all dressed up for Keith Holden's wedding

CAMDEN NEW JOURNAL

Thursday, 10 March 1994   No 614
An independent paper. Free to 55,000 homes and businesses
Also at selected newsagents, price 15p
ADVERTISING (071) 482 1960 (24 hours)
EDITORIAL (071) 485 8207 FAX (071) 485 3519

20 years of market madness!

THE PEOPLE who launched a thousand shops and stalls held a reunion
on Saturday to celebrate the opening
20 years ago of one of Europe's top
tourist attractions — Camden Lock.
In the early 1970s empty sheds littered Camden Lock... until Eric
Reynolds opened it as a market.
To celebrate the Lock's 20th birth-

the seventi
Reynold,
Ramen Bh
Huntley Sp
Floss Parn
the Lock in
cut the birth
Picture
Parnell,
Reynolds,

By then I was selling earrings for £25, while others were selling cheap imports for £2.' A few years later Eric Reynolds left Camden Lock, ending nearly twenty five years as market manager and what had been a very successful business partnership with Northside. And what did he learn from his time at the market? 'Keep smiling I suppose. I learnt to deal with people, although not always that successfully. But I've gone on to work with a lot of the same people, I have learned to be loyal and stay with them, and if I'm in a big hurry to get something done then there are people I can hire.'

Once Eric left, Alan Jones took over as market manager and so began the third chapter in the history of Camden Lock. Like his predecessor, Alan and his team had their share of conflict with stallholders. 'You had to do a lot of arse licking,' says one. 'If you fell out with management or if you turned up ten minutes late you were told, "take a week off next week." I had been there for six years every day and every weekend, I was away for six weeks after my mum died and when I came back they had a go at me for being away for so long!' Another stallholder had a permanent spot in the area where people gathered in the morning to get a pitch. 'I worked one day, another woman did the other. One morning I arrived and put up the stall and in front of everyone I was embarrassed and made to take it down. It was punishment for the stall not having been put up the previous day, when the other woman hadn't shown up, which wasn't my fault at all. I was close to tears, they'd stood and watched me put together the frame and put up the tarpaulin and drag all the bags in and *then* they told me to take it down.' As another stallholder told the press, 'It's the turning up regularly no matter what, that gets you a permanent pitch. I'd have to have died or to have won the Lottery not to show up.' Alan, like Eric before him, had 'a job no one really wanted to do', says bookseller Chris.

'There were lots of uptight sellers, it's an impossible job and you need to be a bit brutal to do it, someone will always be disappointed.' There were frequent arguments over space – some which Alan describes as legitimate, such as complaints about a stallholder playing loud music, and others petty, such as 'so and so has a t-shirt hanging over my stall by two inches'. 'I would try to encourage a handshake between protagonists,' he says, 'sometimes even a hug, because I saw the noble side; these were self-employed individuals working all hours in all weathers.'

Camden was still known for its 'street cred'. 'His Purpleness, the rock star once known as Prince, has chosen ever-hip Camden as the site for his first European shop and the coolest hangout for fans,' reported the *Daily Express* in 1994. However within two years New Power Generation Store on Chalk Farm Road had closed. For some traders life at the end of the 90s had got a bit more cut-throat. June Carroll, now divorced from Eric after a ten-year marriage, decided to leave, after fifteen years at the Lock. 'It was a good honest endeavour until the late 80s. Then it became a question of turn up, scrub up, go home, with a feeling of dread that I had to do the next week as well.' For Donovan, the problem was 'More jewellery people came in, a lot of people travelled to Thailand, we called them weekend warriors, they'd been backpacking to Thailand for six months, got a stall for a day, and sold things cheap. There was more competition and people got priced out. Selling at the Lock wasn't a hobby; people were travelling, selling, and then buying houses. I bought one in Jamaica.'

The rock star formerly known as Prince briefly opened up a shop for fans near the Lock, on Chalk Farm Road

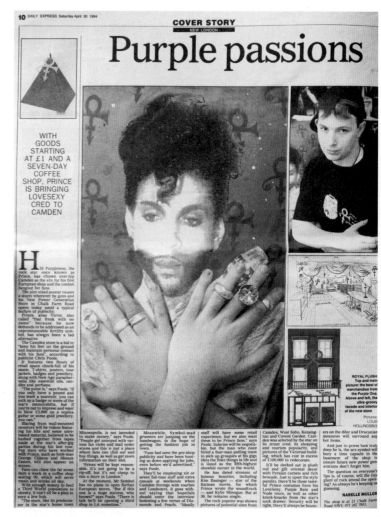

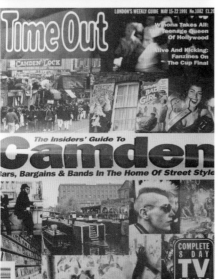

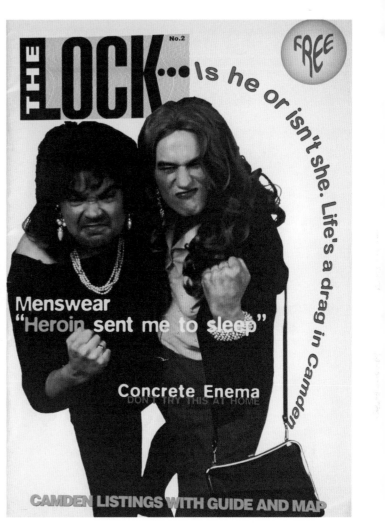

The Lock often featured in magazines. Top left: a 1991 edition of *City Limits*; bottom: *Time Out*. It also had its own magazine: issue number 2 of *The Lock* in 1995, a free Camden listings magazine

10. The Market in the 21st Century

You got a fake tattoo of skull and cross bones
We bought a 10 quid bag of magic mushrooms
We ate our fish and chips under the bridge in Camden Town
In Camden Town
From 'Camden Town', Michelle Featherstone, 2009

The beginning of the twenty-first century saw some difficult times in Camden Town; there were several violent assaults on the Regent's Canal towpath and some gruesome discoveries in the water, just as there had been in Victorian times. The area also became known as a centre for drug dealing; until the early 1990s the towpaths had been locked at night, but now they were left open, leading to what Maggie French describes as 'graffiti and hooliganism and people drinking all night'. She remembers frequent reports of bodies found in the canal between Little Venice and Hackney, sometimes as many as one a month. In 2001 a ten-year-old boy fishing found parts of a woman's body in holdall bags, the following years would see a fatal stabbing on the towpath, and a young man shot in the head in Gilbeys Yard, reportedly as a result of drug turf war.

Drug paraphernalia such as pipes had always been on sale in the market, but now things had got out of hand. At the end of 2002, 200 police made a dramatic rush-hour swoop on what the press described as 'Camden Lock Bridge', with a helicopter and riverboat police. According to police, it had got to the stage where 'one man was walking down the street shouting "happy hour, get your ganja at knockdown prices"'. The swoop resulted in forty-two arrests and the seizure of six kilos of cannabis, but by the following summer the dealers were back. One website offering a 'travellers guide to getting high' promised, 'contacts are easily made in Camden Town…go to the markets…and the stallholders will likely give you a hand to find a hook up.'

The beginning of the twenty-first century saw some difficult times in Camden Town, but the Lock remained a trendy place to hang out on a weekend

Maggie remembers people selling drugs on Camden High Street. They would say, "skunk weed" to everyone who went past, it was like a catch phrase, every day, every night. Europeans got quite scared. I told one man, "I'm an old woman, why would you think I'd want to buy your drugs?" And he said, "you'd be surprised; a lot of my customers are men in suits with briefcases."'

'There was a real drug menace,' agrees manager Alan Jones. 'We had to confront them because traders were really intimidated, there were fights outside the market and my security guards had to put themselves on the line. I was put in a cell twice; arrested because of a fight with drug dealers. They were selling drugs on the bridge and they insulted my mother so there was a fight and the police arrested me, they had to. I spent a night in the cells at Albany Road and at Kentish Town, but the police were very nice to me. I also went to court as a prosecution witness, because other people were too frightened. Drug dealers still say to me, "Hello Mr Alan!"' He says Lock management took a very strong line on keeping drug paraphernalia off the stalls, 'as it would have been the height of hypocrisy to be needling the police to do something about the growing drug menace while allowing that stuff to be sold on our stalls, but having said that it was a continual struggle to keep the cannabis t-shirts at arm's length'.

However, things did then improve. 'When you get a huge number of young people then low life will find their clients,' says officer manager Cathy Palmer, 'but then the police and British Waterways took it seriously.' Waterways paid for private security on the towpath until round 9pm and that, says Maggie, 'really cleaned it up'. But the situation was enough to make some long-term traders leave. 'The Lock got seedy,' says one, 'to begin with it was just people selling a bit of weed, then I was offered crack. They cleared King's Cross of dealers, and they then moved to Camden and the vibe turned.'

Despite its rough reputation, Camden continued to see the establishment of new luxury apartments around the Lock. Gilbey House offered porterage, gym and sauna, while Weatherspoons opened a large pub at the Ice Wharf opposite the back of the market, not far from the old 1830s ice wharf.

Such were the crowds that came to the Lock that Camden Town Tube Station, already closed for entrance on Sunday afternoons, was said to be unable to cope. Plans were announced for a £130 million development, with a seven-storey tower consisting of flats and shops, thus threatening the future of Buck Street and Electric Ballroom markets. There was a public inquiry, and the plans were dropped. Another development also met with fierce resistance, when the owners of the Stables Market next to the Lock announced a £22 million plan to convert the old horse hospital, tunnels and basement into a three-level shopping arena. Traders objected, saying it would destroy the historic character of the site, much as they had opposed earlier developments at Camden Lock.

At the same time the New Economics Foundation published a survey on 'clone town Britain', concerned at the rate at which high street shops were being replaced by chain stores. Although Camden High Street didn't score too badly on the clone scale, researcher Ruth Potts explained that when entrepreneurs revive an area they are often priced out as big retail moves in. 'The same is currently happening in Camden Lock, where a mix of vibrant independent retails have created a bit of a buzz. Such a buzz in fact, that the likes of Gap and Starbucks are beginning to move in.' Starbucks had now opened a store in the old lock-keeper's cottage and some residents were furious when it fitted lights to the outside of the Grade II listed building.

Other suggested developments were less controversial, however. British Waterways and Transport for London came up with plans for the Regent's Canal to carry freight again, by re-introducing commercial barges between Camden Town and Slough Arm, a route without locks. An initial fleet of twenty-six boats would take up to 4,000 lorry trips off the capital's roads, carrying waste and aggregate, with each barge holding 100

tonnes, the equivalent of five juggernauts. However, the plans are yet to materialise, much to the disappointment of canal campaigners.

Meanwhile, life at the Lock continued and stallholders remember several national and international events having an impact on trade. 'The year 2000 was amazing,' says Janice Issitt. 'It was a really great Christmas, but the next year things changed. I was at the market the day the World Trade Center was hit, and there was no one there at all. We weren't allowed TV and we weren't really allowed to play music, but somehow someone heard what had happened on the radio and told us, and I remember the shock of it all.'

The following years saw a serious drop in takings for Janice, due to a combination of reasons. 'When the Japanese had money then things were good, it was always a fantastic day if a couple of Japanese people shopped at my stall, but then they stopped coming. With the London bombings and then the foot and mouth outbreak in 2007, the tourist trade came to a full stop. And it was always tourists who came to the Lock anyway, not the British, they only came at Christmas.'

The Waterbus boats lost twenty percent of their passengers after the London bombs, when on 7 July 2005 a series of suicide attacks killed fifty-two people, with three bombs detonated on London tubes and a fourth on a double decker bus, injuring over 700 people. Alan Jones remembers shortly afterwards, 'a man came to the market as a casual with Union Jack t-shirts saying 'we are not afraid', and I thought, that's what we want here, that we collectively are not afraid. He was given a stall; I still have a t-shirt now, although he didn't do that well.'

International brands moved into Camden Town: Starbucks opened a store in the old lock-keeper's cottage

However Cathy Palmer says the closing of the tube on Sundays had a greater effect than 9/11 or local bomb scares. She compares market traders to farmers: 'I would ask someone who had been there for twenty or thirty years, "are times good?" And they would always say the same thing, "Oh they're all right." Like farmers, they never have a good year. It's a cash business, and that was always hanging over them.' 'If it's not a bomb,' says Alan, 'it will be something else, the management, the weather, the tube being closed, the London Marathon, there is always a reason why a trader is not doing so well.'

Dave forced to tighten his belt

by TONY NEAL

Camden Lock is losing one of its founding fathers – and finest craftsmen. But David Bristow is buckling down to a new beginning

A LEATHER craftsman who helped pioneer Camden Lock is quitting the market after 26 years.

Veteran trader David Bristow is giving up his belt shop in the West Yard to continue his business from his home at Anson Road, Tufnell Park.

David, 57, says he has reluctantly decided to leave the Lock because of escalating rents, diminishing demand for his skills and his desire for a more relaxed lifestyle.

"My grandmother and uncle used to do leather work and in the old days it used to be taught as part of the curriculum in many schools," he said.

"I picked it up from a friend. I had no special training – just hours of patient trial and error. Then I started up in the market with just a stall," he recalled.

"In those early days, the market was a very different place. I remember one day in

priced from £10-£20 for plainer belts to £50-£100 for more elaborate and embossed designs.

He also stocks larger sized belts unavailable elsewhere and offers a made-to-measure service. Over the years he has won some famous clients, ranging from Dave Mason of Pink Floyd, Terry Gilliam and Terry Jones from the Monty Python team, to Bill Oddie and Valerie Singleton in his Blue Peter days.

"I think one of my more unusual orders was to make an elaborate belt featuring a dragon's head with fire spouting out of it for Iron Maiden's drummer.

"He was delighted with it, but friends who went to the concert and saw the video said

work more than four months of the year just to pay my rent, business rates and service charges, let alone buying my materials, tools and employing two part-time staff workers," he said.

"Another factor is that the market has changed. People seem to expect mass-produced goods these days and don't seem to be so appreciative of quality handcrafted goods which can be distinctive and also last a lifetime.

David reckons around 70 per cent of his business comes from regular customers.

"That's why I've decided I can work from home and sell by mail order and the internet.

"I shall be packing up shop in mid-November and am looking forward to getting a bit

David Bristow's belt and bag business has fallen victim to fashion. *Picture by Ni...*

Lock is hell for leathe...

DAVID Bristow will tan his last hide next month at the Camden Lock workshop he has run for the past 26 years.

In that time his intricate leather bags and belts have adorned the waists of heavy metal legends Iron Maiden and several members of the Monty Python team.

But Mr Bristow, 57, has decided to shut up shop because he says there is no longer a demand for his style of handcrafted goods

leader and writer Adi Da Samraj.

Mr Bristow said: "I have mixed feelings about leaving. I have made some really good friends among the traders but now it's time to move on.

"The average Camden Lock visitor is now a teenage fashion victim and that is not the market for my products. I think the image of the Lock now is that it's a bit tacky and all the stallholders are being tarred with the same brush."

for his loyal customer f and sell via his website.

Mr Bristow swapped hi in insurance for the hip and became one of the ves stallholders at the Lock in 1

"When I started the Lo really just the remans of a yard," he said. "There we about 30 market stalls and ter there would be more than there were customers.

"Although I'll miss m here, what I'm most l forward to is ringing my

Some sellers felt driven out by an increase in rent and a shift in what people wanted to buy. 'It was getting to the stage when I couldn't afford to make bags any more,' says leatherworker David Bristow. 'There was so much tourist stuff that people expected to pay £40 for a bag whereas my bags took a day to make, they were stitched by hand, and sold for £120. Mine will last for fifteen years, but there's no use telling them that. It's the same for all craft people, customers are used to mass-produced stuff that only lasts a couple of years.'

But people still queued up for pitches, especially food sellers keen for a stall in the West Yard. In the early years of the twenty-first century this yard 'was dead as a doornail', remembers Alan, 'no one wanted to trade in the week and at the weekend it was junk t-shirts. People didn't want to be there because no one else wanted to be there. There was no food then at all, but then a woman called Crystal who sold Nigerian food suddenly said to me one Sunday, "I have some food left over; I want to see if I can sell it on Monday." It was mid-summer, there were 300 hungry journalists working at the Interchange Building (a former gin warehouse and now the home of Associated Press), and in a couple of weeks others said they wondered if they could sell food on Monday and Tuesday as well!'

138

Left Leatherworker David Bristow felt driven out by the increase in cheap, mass-produced 'tourist stuff'
Above The Lock made headline news in 2008 when a fire broke out at the nearby Canal Street Market and blazed through the wooden stalls

In 2008 the Lock made national news when, on the night of 9 February, a fire broke out at Canal Street Market on the east side of Chalk Farm Road opposite the Lock, and blazed through the wooden stalls. A hundred firefighters fought for hours to contain the fire, thousands of people were evacuated from nearby homes, bars and pubs, including the now iconic Hawley Arms, which had become famous for its regulars such as Amy Winehouse, Kate Moss and Pete Doherty, and around ninety market stalls were badly damaged.

Journalist Michael Hann argued it was no great loss. 'No local people ever went to the Hawley Arms or the Lock market. Why on earth would we care?' Instead he said people in the area hoped it would lead to 'a thinning of the crowds: fewer continental teens in their anoraks, shuffling in lumbering herds', attracted to what they saw as a drink-

and-drugs theme park for bored teenagers. 'How many Camden locals ever felt the need to buy cannabis-flavoured lollies or goth platform boots?' Developers, he said, had been eyeing the site for years and now they would probably get their hands on it.

While many would say locals have always used the Hawley Arms and shopped and worked at the market, Hann was right about developers. As a result of the fire, several buildings were demolished, including the old Caernarvon Castle pub, and in 2011 arguments about redevelopment flared up once more, this time over Hawley Wharf, earmarked for development by the Regent's Canal Group back in the 1960s, which had been partly destroyed in the blaze. Developers Stanley Sidings promised 900 jobs would be created, as well as a new infant school, but locals weren't impressed. Councillors threw out the plans in March 2012 and Ian Shacklock of the Friends of Regent's Canal praised the council for rejecting an application for 'a bulky development that would have undermined the canal as an open space'.

Above Fire-fighters fought for hours to contain the blaze and thousands of people were evacuated
Right The site of the old Caernarvon Castle pub was demolished as a result of the fire

Meanwhile, in December 2011, there had been a change in ownership at Camden Lock. The *Financial Times* reported, 'a private equity-backed vehicle has taken control of Camden Lock Market, the popular shopping, cultural and tourist attraction often cited as the heartland of London's alternative music culture.' While vacancy rates on UK high streets were soaring, Camden Lock had a 'backlog of tenants waiting to take up space in the canal-flanked yards that were once used to store timber brought into London by barge'. In comparison, business at other street markets in Camden was dire: a Town Hall report found an average occupancy rate of just forty-five percent. In Queen's Crescent

Market, only one in five pitches were hired out on a Saturday, while Chalton Street and Leather Lane were faring even worse.

The *Financial Times* reported that Urban Market Company had bought the one-acre site for 'between £30m and £40m', in a joint venture between a number of parties including Northside shareholders, Peter Wheeler and Bill Fulford, the original founders of Camden Lock, retail developers Milligan, and Brockton Capital, a specialist real estate private equity fund. And one of the leading players is none other than David Marks, a partner at Brockton, who started out as a sixteen-year-old entrepreneur selling bootleg tapes on the bridge outside the market.

'In these times a market stall is the ultimate in start-ups,' he says. 'You don't need an office, a lock up, twelve computers…if you want to sell something, try your luck with a stall. You know 30 million people are passing through there, and you'll find out if you're any good, do people want what you're selling?' When Northside decided to sell, 'they didn't want a faceless developer,' says David, so he personally wrote the offer, stressing 'we have the capital, you have the history and the expertise, and then there is the third element, the buzz and the vibe that is Camden.'

To David, the market is an important piece of London 'and you can't mess it up. It's a unique setting, off the street, in a yard, over a canal; there are no cars, just cobbled courtyard. There are so many tribes here, whether Japanese fashion tourists or Barcelona fans coming here after a match against Arsenal…it's a real mix of people who come through. The place has history and community and a vibe, and you have to look after it. But it also has to move forward or become stale. With an asset like Camden you have to stand back and ask, what was this like ten, twenty years ago? What will it be like in ten years' time? It needs to be the most interesting place in London to hang out on a weekend.' And what if someone had told him some twenty-five years ago, while he was selling bootleg tapes on the bridge, that someday this would all be his? David laughs. 'I was sixteen, I would have been like, "what?" I wanted to play for West Ham and go to Ibiza; I didn't even have an idea of owning a market.'

11. The Regent's Canal & Camden Town Today

It's a blisteringly hot Saturday in May, a week before the Queen's Diamond Jubilee celebrations, and the towpaths of the Regent's Canal are packed with revellers. People sunbathe and dip their toes in the water, tourists take pictures of each other on their mobile phones. There's the clink of ice as a group of visitors outside the Ice Wharf Café raise their glasses. Two children on the towpath lick ice cream, bought perhaps from the Chin Chin Laboratorists, billed as Europe's first Liquid Nitrogen Ice-Cream Parlour, 'blending haute cuisine with performance art in a celebration of gastronomic graphic design'.

The Regent's Canal today is a thriving leisure route through London
Right The annual Canalway Cavalcade at Little Venice

It's certainly a long way from Carlo Gatti's Victorian penny ices, in the days when ice was imported from Norway and stored in huge wells along the Regent's Canal. The waterway then was a bustling commercial route, with barges and narrowboats carrying goods from far and wide. Now the Regent's Canal, which started a series of bicentennial celebrations in 2012, is a thriving leisure route, with three annual festivals held along its banks, the Canalway Cavalcade at Little Venice in May, the Shoreditch Festival in July and the Angel Canal Festival at City Road Lock in September. And now there are new guardians of the Canal, the Canal & River Trust, which took over British Waterways' 2,000 miles of canals and rivers in England and Wales in 2012, and which has promised to 'give people a greater role in the running of their local waterways'.

On the roving bridge tourists gather to watch three boats travel slowly through Hampstead Road Lock, the site of Congreve's failed hydro-pneumatic lock, where the water rushes though the gates as loud as a waterfall. The last boat glides through, its roof crowded with potted plants, a bicycle, a ladder, and a waving Union Jack.

The old monkey boats, once inhabited by impoverished families, have been replaced by new, pretty houseboats, and such is the demand that there is a severe shortage of local moorings. Blomfield Road near Little Venice is the most prestigious site in London. Around 2,000 people live permanently on houseboats in London, and on the Regent's Canal fixed barges include a floating café, art gallery, puppet theatre, several bookshops and a Chinese restaurant. The twenty-first century has seen a resurgence in canal life, and houseboats are regarded by many as the most sustainable way to live, although they're not necessarily cheap; a one-bed houseboat can cost £110,000, while a mooring lease can be £8,000 a year. But they have even been seen as a possible solution to the housing crisis.

Down at Dingwalls Wharf inlet, people queue to board a Waterbus boat, ready for a trip to Little Venice. Back in the 1960s, the Regent's Canal Group urged for better provision for pleasure boats; today Maggie French has turned the Waterbus company into one of the biggest operators of its kind in Europe. It has a fleet of four boats, three of which are on the national register of historic ships, and she's the only woman who runs such a business single-handed. The majority of her customers are British, mainly from London and the southeast, but there's been an increase in Spanish and Italians in the past two years. 'We've seen a real urge, it's easier to get to England by train, a lot of Germans come by Eurostar and since St Pancras Station opened we get a lot more French.'

On a very busy day the four boats leave every half an hour from 10am-6pm, carrying everyone from school groups to international celebrities. 'Joan Collins was delightful, she went to the zoo with her grandchildren and she didn't expect not to pay, which is what a lot of famous people do, but she paid by cheque. Gwyneth Paltrow hired a boat for a children's party. We've had Suggs, Paul Weller more than once, various comedians and actors, and often TV presenters film from a boat.'

Weather can still be a problem, especially if the canal freezes in January or February, or sometimes as early as November, and people still throw things from bridges, such as bricks and pallets. Once when Maggie was steering a boat under a bridge by Prince Albert Road someone hurled a bucket of maggots. Others have thrown cans with urine, children kick footballs onto the boats, and even a lit firework. 'They don't understand it can kill people,' says Maggie. 'But things aren't as bad as they were five years ago.'

Roy Walker, whose father Paddy launched the *Jenny Wren* back in the 1960s, sits at a table on the towpath opposite Hawley Wharf, facing his floating restaurant *My Fair Lady*. Every five minutes he breaks off to answer his phone, fielding inquiries from people who want to book a trip. But the demand, he says, is not linked to the market. 'The markets have had a detrimental effect on the boat business. People don't want to fight their way through throngs of tourists to get here. But when they do, it's an escape from the madness.'

He doesn't support the plans for Hawley Wharf or the redevelopment of the tube station. 'There will be some sort of development around here, but I would like it if they try to keep to a proper scale and preserve at least some open space. It will get to the stage

Top left Maggie French has turned the Waterbus into one of the biggest operators of its kind in Europe
Top right Travelling by boat is 'an escape from the madness': Roy Walker with his boat the *Jenny Wren*
Bottom left A reveller at the annual Angel Canal festival held at City Road Lock
Bottom right Boats at Little Venice celebrate the Queen's Diamond Jubilee

'Camden Town is world famous now': scenes from the High Street

where the open markets are all retail.'

Camden Town has grown enormously since its birth as a five-street town in the 1790s: it now has a population of just over 26,000 and according to the borough's council has a 'youthful energy' with 'a real mix of social and economic conditions'. To Jack Whitehead, who remembers the town in the 1920s, the place has changed so much 'it bears no real relation to the bedraggledness that it was. Camden planners have seen the market as a cash cow, but the great thing is they have stuck to height and refused to have a tower block: if they had allowed one then it would have produced devastation. The market has brought in the big firms, in the past you could get a shop opposite the tube for tuppence ha'penny rent, and now they are worth enormous amounts of money. I'm always expecting the market to collapse, because how can they keep up the enthusiasm? But it does seem to be a fun place. Camden Town is world famous now.'

'Camden 250 years ago was a mud bath,' says Simon Pitkeathley, Chief Executive of Camden Town Unlimited, a Business Improvement District formed in 2006. 'It exists today because of road, rail and water; all the horse tunnels and the Interchange Building were all about the movement of goods. The Interchange itself was a version of a market, while the original market exists because of the proposed ring road: it was built out of a dead space.' He says there are mixed views on whether the markets have helped preserve the Regent's Canal. 'Traditionalists want it how it was, they don't want young people eating food, stopping them walking down the towpath, but you can't stop change.' And as for Starbucks, 'who else will maintain the lock-keeper's cottage? Compromise is better than disrepair.'

To Simon, 'progress is inevitable' and he says the old antique stalls so popular in the 1970s disappeared not because of development but 'because you can no longer buy tat in Yorkshire and sell it with a big mark-up at the Lock, and people got wise to that. You can't now find a little village junk shop that doesn't understand the value of what it has. Markets are commercial beasts and they respond to *the* market.'

While physically Camden might look very different, and while a lot of the character of the town has come from the market and the music scene, 'it hasn't changed that much over the last thirty years. It's often said that it's a melting pot, but it's not, it's layers of people existing on top of each other. There are tourists and punks and goths, people come for music, others come for expensive nights out at places like Gilgamesh in the Stables, and they are very different from the people who come to the Lock on a Saturday. It's interesting how little they mix, it's more of a strata, but they do happily co-exist.'

Camden is still well known for its music. The four pubs that were built during the construction of the Regent's Canal were the key starting point for the area's music scene, explains Simon, particularly the Dublin Castle with its long tradition of Irish players. Canal and then railway workers brought a live music culture over from Ireland and this was 'hugely important. When the music scene started happening in the 60s there was a ready-made environment with pubs and public address systems, it was an ideal environment for music to flourish.' The 1970s saw the birth of several new venues including Dingwalls, The Music Machine and the Electric Ballroom, by the 80s Camden was 'the place where music was happening', and this evolved eventually into the Brit pop of the 90s. Some music management companies are still based in Camden, such as The Who's and Robert Palmer's. 'If you're plotting Camden's evolution,' says Simon, 'I would say it's becoming more like Soho than Shoreditch,

Camden Town is 'layers of people existing on top of each other...tourists, punks, goths, they happily co-exist'

it's old enough now, it's riding the waves of cool, it comes and goes, but Camden is more like the grande dame than a young pretender.'

Compared with forty years ago, however, it's now 'quite an affluent area, to some extent people can't afford to live here, and my problem is finding space for start-ups. The major employer is not the markets, we have Asos down the road, French Connection, Hugo Boss, all headquarters of reasonably large fashion houses which have moved here in the last twenty years; there are also lots of publishing houses, as well as numerous PR agencies.' But Simon hopes the growth of Camden in the future will be less tourist-focused, 'I would love London to rediscover Camden.'

Three of the four pubs built during the construction of the Regent's Canal still exist today: The Dublin Castle (centre) in particular was a key starting point for the local music scene

Top right The Hawley Arms, once popular with stallholders and now known for its celebrity clientele

12. The Market Today & Beyond

'Trying to define Camden Lock is like putting your thumb on a ball of mercury,' says Will Fulford, son of one of the Lock founders, as he sits outside Café Chula in the West Yard, watching the world go by. 'Just when you think you've worked out what it is, it morphs into something more interesting. It was built from the ground up, without subsidies or handouts, and it works on an economic and a social level in equal measure. There is conflict, but there's also resolution, friendships and marriages; it's a very rich social space and is there another commercial form that does all of that?' Today Will is Head of New Business Development, but it's taken him a few decades to appreciate the place. 'I was completely oblivious to the fact dad was one of the owners of Camden Lock while growing up, I never gave it a second thought, I just had to come here and hang around the office and wait for him to finish and take me somewhere interesting…'

When Will was around eight, he did try his luck on a stall one winter with his older brother and sister, selling pet Christmas stockings. 'We hardly sold anything the first four days and then on the very last day a man came and bought them all, he said he had thirty ferrets.' Despite this experience, the market still didn't mean much to Will. He went to university to study marine biology, and later did a business degree. By then weekday trade at the Lock was growing, and when a part-time temporary job came up for a mid-week market manager, Will applied in order to pay off his student loans. 'That's when I began to realise the Lock was something very special. There are so many abstract things to a site's success, like atmosphere, colour and vitality, but how do you measure them? There is such a diverse section of London here, people from different economic backgrounds, from every religion and nationality, all with different norms, values and beliefs. People lose stereotypes working at a market, they see people are doing what

'There are so many abstract things to a site's success…atmosphere, colour and vitality'

152

they do and that they deserve to earn money the same as they do. This is responsible capitalism in action.'

Intrigued at the Lock's success, Will went back to university where he took an MA in Urban Regeneration, writing his dissertation on street markets. First he examined the existing literature on public spaces from the 1950s onwards, in which experts like William H. Whyte and Jan Gehl have identified three elements that build great spaces. The first is density – there needs to be plenty of people but without overcrowding, what Whyte calls 'self-congestion', a lot of people choosing to be in the same space at the same time. The second is diversity – both of people and function. The third is social encounters, whether buying something from a trader, a chance meeting with someone you know but haven't planned to meet, like a neighbour, or eye contact and a fleeting smile with a stranger. But Will found there is hardly anything written on markets in public space literature, 'yet they've been around for 7,000 years and markets are where we developed the foundations of our civilization: written language; money and mathematics.'

For his thesis, he looked at Queen's Market in Newham, East London and Union

'Markets are where we developed the foundations of our civilisation': scenes from the Lock today

Square Greenmarket in New York. He measured density, diversity and social interactions, and found that with the latter most were functional. 'At a supermarket it would be similar, but there functional encounters are "heads down", the focus is on the task of shopping. But the range and type at a market is so much richer. Most will be hardly noticeable, but others will last half an hour or more. People talk about the weather, their children's schools, how to cook a strange looking vegetable, it can be nothing to do with the exchange of money.'

After Will finished his MA, he set up a company called Spaceworks with his father. 'I wondered why there weren't more markets like Camden Lock, and we wanted to see if we could do it somewhere else, to spread the philosophy.' At the same time John Milligan, Chief Executive Officer at Milligan Retail, was redeveloping Maremagnum, a waterside site in Barcelona, during which he handed out questionnaires to locals. One question was, 'where would you most like to shop outside of Barcelona?' The response was New York, Paris…and then Camden Lock. It wasn't long before John contacted Spaceworks and together they formed the Urban Market Company (UMC) and began looking for

opportunities in regional cities such as Manchester, Bath and Glasgow. But Will says it proved hard to sell the idea of market-based developments to financial institutions: can you really let market stalls on handshakes, and what if everyone one day just decided not to turn up? UMC eventually joined forces with Brockton Capital to buy the Lock as 'a seed asset for future developments' and they'll be looking at other market projects together, both in London and nationally.

While Will says there has been growth in markets in the UK, in areas where they are most needed, the traditional street markets are 'dying year by year, it's a tragedy. There is more competition now, the pound shops killed off street markets. They are in decline; they have been undervalued and misunderstood by central and local government, who have lost the skills and expertise to run them. Traders leave because they're not doing so well, then customers leave, and the next generation of traders isn't coming through. To a local authority, a market costs money rather than making money. It's not their fault though, traditional street markets are bound by all kinds of legislation that would kill off any kind of business.'

A recent report by the National Association of British Market Authorities found that

The Din performing at a L.U.V Camden gig in Dingwalls Gallery
Top Left 'What's going on at Camden Lock is very contemporary': the brightly lit exterior of the Market Hall

retail market performance is similar to the rest of the high street; trading conditions are tough. In a survey of 261 markets, nearly half of the operators reported a decrease in income. However, outdoor markets, farmers' markets and privately operated markets appear to be doing better than indoor and local authority managed markets.

'People ask if being a stallholder is a real job,' says Will, 'but they are running a business and they have to know every part of that business. It's the ultimate in entrepreneurialism. What is going on at Camden Lock, I love it. It's a link to the past, but it's also very contemporary.' Will, along with Gary Prosser and Manny Montanaro, has now brought music back to the original Dingwalls, with the launch of L.U.V Camden, which has hosted free weekly music in Dingwalls Gallery, part of the Market Hall and the site of the original Dingwalls stage.

UMC are now applying for another round of planning permission, aiming for more space. 'Camden Lock is a cycle, of decline and rejuvenation, spikes and plateaus,' says Bill Fulford, 'and in this development we're trying to create new life. The first phase of Camden Lock worked brilliantly for the market but the making element got squeezed out; in this development we want to get all four elements going again, craft units, market, restaurants and music, especially the workshop element.' The plans entail 'a fairly major development', still subject to public consultation and planning permission, but the focus is on 'the areas that don't really work' and they're talking to art colleges about how to showcase young people's work. 'The story of Camden Lock is where it's gone and where it's going,' says Bill. 'We want more of the work/creative element, that's our ambition, and we're great believers in low-cost start-up opportunities. There are different stages and different pressures; the story of Camden Lock is one of evolution.'

Up in the Lock's offices Jake Emms is surveying the scene out of the window. A former landscape gardener, he started as a market manager three years ago. 'I enjoy the atmosphere and the challenges. I see the same traders every day, they're my friends. It's like a soap opera out there, there's drama every day, from relationships to trade disputes to nit picking. It's the human race at its liveliest.'

There are now 280 stalls at Camden Lock, as well as fifty-four retail shops, twenty offices/studios, and four eateries/restaurants. Ten percent of stalls are still kept for casuals, and would-be traders assemble in Camden Lock Place every weekend at 8.45am, 9.15am on weekdays. A weekday stall costs between £15 and £30 depending on location, £45 at weekends. A large food stall in the West Yard costs £150 a day.

Some stallholders are reluctant to talk, they don't want their names publicised, or to be asked about their turn-over, but Hasan Kaygusuz is happy to chat. He's been here for seven years and was one of the first to sell food midweek. 'There were twenty-one food stalls at the weekend, midweek I was the only one here. But I was determined. Now there are sometimes thirty stalls midweek selling food and drink.' His stall is called Ala Turko Kebab, and as he talks he threads marinated chunks of chicken onto kebab sticks. Born in Turkey, Hasan arrived in the UK as an eight-year-old. He has fifteen years experience in the restaurant trade and used to run a kebab takeaway shop in the East End. Then he decided to try his luck at Camden Lock. 'I love it here, it's so vibrant; this guy here – ' he points to his neighbour, 'is from Spain, he's selling food right next to me and we get along really well. Life is very competitive on the high street, there's more understanding here. Tourists have got positive energy, they smile at me and I smile back at them.'

Kim Le is another successful food seller. She started at Camden Lock eleven years ago and along with her husband runs Kim's Vietnamese Food Hut in Dingwalls Gallery, just off Camden Lock Place. Now thirty-seven, she arrived in England from Vietnam as a four-year-old; she learnt to cook from her mother and aunt and later managed a Chinese take away in Dockland. In 1996 she started selling food at the Stables: 'I had no money, I had just had a baby and just got married, and an opportunity came up when I saw a stall

'It's like a soap opera out there':
Jake Emms, one of today's market managers
Top right 'Life is very competitive on the High Street, there's more understanding here': Hasan Kaygusuz
Bottom right 'I put love in my food': Kim Le

being advertised.' Her father, meanwhile, was already running a food stall opposite Inverness Street Market, where Kim worked part-time, and 'all the traders were going to his stall to eat.'

She says such was her success at the Stables, where she worked with her mother, that 'I put my father out of business! Then traders from the Lock were buying food at the Stables and I was asked if I could move to the Lock.'

She's been operating from the same site ever since. In 2006 *The Guardian* named her business as one of the fifty healthiest places to eat in London; she's been featured in *Time Out*, and in 2010 and 2011 won the King of Camden Best Food award organised by Camden Town Unlimited.

She attributes her success to putting 'love in my food'. Eighty percent of her trade is regulars, 'people who live around here, I see their children grow up.' She also has a tourist base, many of whom return every time they're in England. 'There is a German couple who come twice a year and a Norwegian family who always come and then tell their friends. Some French people came and I was in their guide book! Camden Lock has been really good to me. There is a lot of competition, I have had problems with people copying my food and taking photos of my menu, but I stick to what I know. The managers here are great, they know I won't stand here and moan about not making money; I just get on with it.'

Traders at Camden Lock still sell a variety of wares, from handmade jewellery, soaps and clothing, to fifty-seven varieties of doughnut, and 'Camden-produced bamboo-fibre and earth-neutral meaningless T-shirts'. Products and souvenirs featuring Camden Lock are numerous, and the bridge sign appears on fridge magnets, postcards, t-shirts, bags, and travelcard holders. 'It's all a bit unstoppable isn't it?' asks architect John Dickinson, who feels his Victorian-inspired Market Hall 'has been taken over by signage; people paint things the wrong

colours and stick things on, it's all been so randomised that I've given up. I once said to a colleague, "I don't want it like Disneyworld." And he said, "it's too late, John!" But I'm not one of those who think you can eliminate people from architecture.'

There are still plenty of events at the Lock, whether Easter egg hunts, fashion shows, or pumpkin festivals. In 2012 it was one of the sites chosen for the Olympic Games torch relay. And then there's the old dance hall Dingwalls, still going strong, with recent acts including Mumford and Sons and Foo Fighters. Co-founder Tony Mackintosh recently went back, and found it 'a little smaller and a lot wider, but with a better stage and better presentation'.

The market continues to attract media coverage. Channel 4 ran a week of educational programmes showing young entrepreneurs cutting their teeth at Camden Lock Market, and American Express chose the High Street and the iconic bridge sign for an

Above left Inside the Victorian-inspired Market Hall
Above right The Lock is still a place to source unique items
Right The Lock was chosen as part of the route for the Olympic torch relay

advertisement broadcast internationally featuring Kate Winslet. The Lock has also been the scene of many a movie, including Anthony Minghella's *Breaking and Entering* and Mike Leigh's *Happy-Go-Lucky*.

But many of the market traders from the early days have left the area, and those still living in London say they rarely visit. 'I never go back to Camden,' says Wendy Shuttleworth who worked on a stall in the 80s. 'In the past everything was homemade, these were the days before imports, now it's generic tat that you can buy in Oxford Street.' Former manager Eric Reynolds says the place is 'like a department store, but it remains popular, I drive past and still see streams of people.'

Others insist it's still the place to go to source unique items. Marice Cumber, who had a stall in the late 80s, says the old community has gone. 'It's huge now, we had an intimate experience, it wasn't overwhelming then. But there are still nuggets to be found and my teenage kids think it's fantastic.' 'If I want to buy someone a present of jewellery or a little scarf,' says Claire, who sold clothes from Thailand in the 90s, 'this is where I go. When I was a trader people came to buy clothes, now the focus has shifted to tourists and tourists are not looking to buy a wardrobe. My customers were Camden people. Now you buy products and you don't even know where they're from. At Camden when you bought something there was a person and a story behind it. The Lock is a story of money and development; it's a reflection of globalisation, and the way we travel has changed: in the 60s you could go to Goa in a van, in the 80s people went overland to Bali, now it's the days of mass tourism, and Camden has shifted to suit that.' But her former partner Tony Winter still takes his children along for 'a nice cheap day out. There is more tacky stuff now, but when I went to a wedding recently and my daughter said she wanted a Chinese dress, I knew I could find it down Camden.'

Donovan, who sold jewellery in the 90s, says Camden as a whole is 'all samey samey, especially on the high street, it hasn't got diversity or ingenuity. It's overdose and overkill, they have squeezed every little space into stalls and it's a bit of a blur. Londoners don't shop at Camden; it's like Woolworths at Christmas, that's when local people go to Camden. But my seventeen-year-old daughter loves it!'

However, designer Wayne Hemingway says if he's 'out vintage shopping then we will go to Camden, because contrary to what people say, there's still lots of stuff to buy. I don't know what all the fuss is about. Camden Market has always been cool, independent, thrifty and individual. There is a lot of cheap tat, and a severe lack of editing going on, but there is still plenty of vintage.'

Others agree that while a lot of the goods are mass-produced, there's still a big variety and visitors can always find something quirky. 'I don't think it's changed that much,' says former 'flower girl' Kee, 'people still sell unique, craft things and there are still some of the same shops. They haven't allowed it to get swamped like the rest of Camden; there are still people's own designs. In other areas people are selling identical things stall to stall but Camden Lock is a bit different and better quality, and the food has always been better at Camden Lock, it really is homemade.'

As for the future, some traders are anxious that with the new Lock owners, leases will be shorter and rents will increase. 'Landlords are not interested in ordinary people but in the property aspect,' says leatherworker David Bristow. 'The worse case is it will become gradually more samey and more touristy. And as for what will happen, the honest answer is I don't know, but it will get further away from what it once was. When I went to visit my brother in Sydney we went to a big street market and I could have sworn I was in Camden Lock. There are stalls and products you can find everywhere, some made in sweat shops and brought here and to Sydney and who knows where else. But the landlords have done a great job with these old buildings, and should take a lot of credit for putting things here that harmonise, compared with the hideous glass building at the Stables market.'

Ray and Barbara Bathke who run Village Games have been in the same West Yard corner shop for thirty years. 'It's a mainstream, young people's market now,' says Ray.

'The food has always been better at Camden Lock': a stallholder in the West Yard
Right 'I like the interaction with people': market manager Eamon Stack

'If you want a t-shirt, you come to Camden Lock.' He says many traders feel in turmoil, aware that their old twenty-year leases are about to expire. 'We're negotiating. The developers specialise in shopping malls, they've told us they love us but...' Ray pauses as a fellow trader comes in and asks to borrow a pair of pliers, and then gets up to help a Spanish man on the hunt for a jigsaw with over 2,000 pieces.

Whatever former stallholders think of the market today, they all remember the place with deep affection. It was where friendships were formed, careers launched and lives changed forever. And now there is a new generation of traders eager to see what the future brings, under the watchful eye of the latest market manager Eamon Stack, who with several assistants still goes around collecting money for the stalls, unlike other markets where traders pay in advance. Eamon first started at the market around sixteen years ago. 'My brother Michael worked with Eric and Alan, doing maintenance jobs. I'd come over from Ireland and was working on building sites in London, I was moaning about it to my brother and he said, "get in touch with Eric." Eamon's wife Louise was a trader in the 80s and 90s, selling jewellery and working on the veggie-burger stall, which her brother Paul now runs. 'I like the interaction with people and dealing with them direct,' says Eamon. 'It's a genuine, open market. People want to work, to make a living, and there's no hint of corruption like there is at other markets. It's not faceless, we're there talking to everyone, and we discourage stalls run by staff, we want the owner to be there.'

However, the number of people asking for stalls has fallen, and they're not always full. 'It's a dilemma,' he says, 'can you turn someone away who has the money to pay the rent? But we still prioritise people with good stuff, we're trying to keep the quality up and we offer discounts to people who make their own stock.' He says permanent traders are far more likely to be declaring their income than in the more freewheeling past. But the days of being a magnet for punks are over: 'There are no real punks or goths any more, that's long gone. If you see any young people in full punk gear they will be Polish or Italian. We're a tourist market now. But I don't believe in the idea that there was ever a golden age: nostalgia polishes people's memories. The market is different today, but the idea of everything being handmade in the old days, well they weren't, they were bought in from places like Thailand, people filled suitcases with cheap goods and bought them back. When I was first here people went to Bali and got ethnic jewellery for nothing and sold it hand over fist, and this was the only place in London where you could get it. There are fewer English stallholders now, but there are people from all over the world selling their *own* stock.' Eamon gestures down Camden Lock Place. 'These Nepali guys over here are selling things from Nepal, there is a Jamaican trader, someone from Guyana, a Chinese-Brazilian partnership, an Indian, an Israeli…a cross section of this market truly represents London, this is multiculturalism, it's how London now is. Come on,' he urges, 'let's have a walkabout then.'

He sets off down Camden Lock Place and points at a woman just to his right. 'She makes these dresses herself, there's another who sits here with her sewing machine making fisherman pants, there's a man selling customised baseball hats. It's easy to be dismissive, but there is still plenty of original design.' He reaches the end of the lane, strolls past the Market Hall, and turns right before the bridge, still pointing at traders who design their own goods. 'Look at the level of artisanship,' he says admiringly.

Aside from the increase in food stalls, and the variety of nationalities selling goods, another major change has been the introduction of stricter regulation. 'According to the Met police we're the fourth top destination in London!' says Property Manager Keir Emms. He's just come off the phone with the anti-terrorism police who are producing a risk report for Camden in the build-up to the Olympics, and with the Lock a popular tourist attraction the place is a priority.

Keir first came to the Lock as a teenager in the mid 80s to buy ripped 501 jeans and

listen to music. 'I saw Spacemen 3 in the old Dingwalls nightclub. It was very loud. I couldn't hear for three days after. The market was just sheds at the front, it was downtrodden and earthy, but it had a nice feel to it.'

In 1996 he began work as an administrative assistant and like many at the Lock, it was a chance piece job that led to a whole new career. 'I had finished university and was doing odd jobs as a painter and decorator, and a friend was working here in the office. The security door was broken and she said "do you want to come and fix it?" It was a £100 job. So I came, someone was going on holiday and they said "do you want to man the office for a couple of weeks?" Basically I stayed on and worked my way up.'

Regulations have got stiffer in recent years, from health and safety, to bomb risk assessment, and operational procedures. Now regular meetings are held about what to do if there is a fire or a bomb – and during a bomb scare on the high street in the late 1990s the site was evacuated in five minutes. But there are difficulties with an old cobbled site, such as creating access for people in wheelchairs, and these days Keir says getting licences for events is not as easy as it was in the past. Another new rule is that stallholders have to be over 16: any younger and they need parental supervision.

'I've seen so many successful businesses come through Camden Lock,' says Keir. 'We're a creative hub and there's a great community spirit, which is the driving force of the place. Being successful is all to do with flair and presentation, that's key. People come for the market experience, they want performance and buzz. You need to have a smile on your face and be proactive; those are the people who will shine."

Epilogue

Where Are They Now?

Bill Fulford and Peter Wheeler still own Northside Developments Limited and remain part owners of Camden Lock.

Bill is a professor at Oxford and Warwick Universities, where he runs programmes in philosophy and medicine.

Peter has been involved in numerous conservation projects, and along with his wife Kay converted Tuckenhay Mill in South Devon into a holiday cottage business with 21 properties, (http://www.tuckenhaymill.co.uk/).

Architect John Dickinson's work includes the refurbishment and conversion of The Royal Victoria Patriotic Building in Wandsworth, Merton Abbey Mills and Gabriel's Wharf.

Wilf Scott is known internationally for his firework displays. His clients have included Pink Floyd, The Rolling Stones, Michael Jackson, and Oasis, and his shows have included The Queen's Ruby Wedding, VE Day, and The Golden Jubilee.

Dingwalls Dance Hall co-founders Tony Mackintosh and John Armit went on to run The Zanzibar, a private members' club in Covent Garden, and the Notting Hill restaurant 192, and along with Tchaik Chassay they founded the literary media members' club The Groucho.

Jeweller Jackie Jones lives in Brighton where she makes sundials, (www.sundialglass.wordpress.com). She has an annual Open House as part of the Brighton Festival and is involved in the management of the British Sundial Society.

'The story of Camden Lock is where it's gone and where it's going...'

Furniture makers Ivan and Judi Foster live in Cornwall where they run Global Home furniture in Truro.

Cathy Palmer lives on the south coast and continues to work with Peter Wheeler. She runs a support group for people with Blepharospasm (a form of Dystonia), a condition which she herself has.

Sarah Jones ran London shops in Basinghall Street and Piccadilly Arcade for 20 years. Her small decorative silver is held in numerous private collections, including those of the Royal Family. She is a Liveryman of the Worshipful Company of Goldsmiths, and a member of the Art Workers' Guild, and continues to make new designs and commissions at her workshop near the City.

Helen Scott Lidgett worked in publishing before co-founding Brunswick Arts, an international corporate communications partnership. In 2010 she was special advisor on charities and arts to Prime Minister Gordon Brown. She passed away in July 2012.

Marc Gerstein's company Lead & Light operates from a purpose-built studio/warehouse in Chalk Farm, supplying tools and materials and producing commissioned stained glass windows to clients including the Royal Family.

Eric Reynolds is based at Trinity Buoy Wharf, where his company Urban Space Management turns

run-down or under-utilised space into retail, workshop and community uses. Projects include Spitalfields Old Fruit & Vegetable Market, the construction of Gabriel's Wharf, and the creation of Merton Abbey Mills.

June Carroll, (www.junepaul.com), ran three Huffs restaurants and bought the Everyman Cinema in Hampstead, north London, the oldest rep cinema in the world, which she later sold.

Marice Cumber worked in art education, before setting up the first dedicated business advice service for creative students and graduates, and then a free legal advice service for creative businesses called 'Own-it'. She now leads on enterprise and entrepreneurship teaching at Ravensbourne College of Design and Communication, and recently set up the Crouch End Festival.

Leatherworker David Bristow returned to the Lock to work at Black Gull Books a couple of days a week, and still makes belts at the leather shop next door. 'I have a workshop at home in the corner of my living room, or rather I have a living room in the corner of my workshop.'

Sculptor Danny Lane is based at a workshop in Willesden, on the banks of the Grand Union Canal. His monumental designs belong to museums and private and corporate collections, including a balustrade of stacked glass for the glass gallery at the Victoria & Albert Museum, two kinetic glass walls at Canary Wharf, and a piece entitled 'Lock, Level, Line' at the redeveloped West Quay at Paddington Basin.

Helen David (www.helenandcolindavid.com) works mainly as a fine artist from a studio in King's Cross along with her husband Colin. Her fashion/textile work is in permanent collections at the Victoria & Albert Museum, the Museum of London and the Art Institute of Chicago. She has held two one-woman art exhibitions.

Ian Morris owns and runs the retail shop Map in Archway, (wwwmapgiftshop.com).

'Lock, Level Line': Danny Lane's sculpture at the redeveloped West Quay at Paddington Basin

Wendy Shuttleworth own and runs The Walpole Restaurant in Ealing, (http://walpole-ealing.co.uk/).

Actress Jacey Sallés is best known for her role as Ramona Ramirez on the hit ITV programme *Cold Feet*. She landed the role three years after leaving the Lock: 'as an actress working at Camden Lock meant I learnt a lot about characters and eccentrics.'

Stevie Stewart works as a fashion, costume, set and production designer. She's designed costumes for international music tours, including Kylie Minogue and Britney Spears, as well as designing for Girls Aloud, Westlife, Cheryl Cole, and the Michael Clark Dance Company.

David Holah is an artist and printmaker, having returned to college to take an MA in printmaking at Camberwell.

Wendy Jones lives quite near Camden and is a novelist.

Joe Swift is a garden designer and TV personality, having presented BBC2's *Gardeners' World* since 1998. He is currently President of the National Gardens Scheme and co-presenter on BBC1's *The Flowerpot Gang*.

Alan Jones lives in Lymington, New Forest. He's moved his boat out of London and with his wife Christine plans to take it towards Bristol and maybe up the Severn.

Janice Issitt lives in Buckinghamshire. Her work includes a new interior design and styling business with Nichole Sleet, (www.thedandelionhouse.co.uk), styling rooms, photo shoots and events. She occasionally sells at vintage fairs around Bucks.

Binh Doan runs Thanh Binh Vietnamese Restaurant on Chalk Farm Road, (http://www.thanhbinhrestaurant.co.uk/).

Chris Overfield owns and runs Black Gull Books at Camden Lock, and in East Finchley.

Everyone looks back at their days at the Lock with fondness. Clockwise from top left: artist Danny Lane, former manager Eric Reynolds, former manager Alan Jones with wife Christine, restaurateur Binh Doan, food seller June Carroll, leatherworker David Bristow and silversmith Sarah Jones

Acknowledgements

Thank you to all the people who generously shared their experiences of Camden Lock, craftspeople and stallholders, staff and management; this book could never have been written without your kind help and support.

It's difficult in a project like this to balance conflicting memories and to pin down exactly what happened when. I'm grateful to the many people who read parts of or all of the manuscript and made vital comments, corrections and suggestions: thanks especially to Peter Wheeler, Cathy Palmer, Ian Shacklock, Maggie French, John Dickinson, and Richard Humphreys (who also provided access to his mountain of paper work).

I'm indebted to those who provided images for the book; Bill Fulford and Peter Wheeler for access to the Northside archives, Eric Reynolds for his photographs and clippings, Cathy Palmer for tracking down the video, Tony Mackintosh for his Dingwalls memorabilia, Dan Carrier at the *Camden New Journal* for photos of the 2008 fire, British Waterways for use of images, and all those who patiently trawled through their old photo albums and cuttings, especially Wilf Scott, who also kindly allowed the use of two of his illustrations, Sarah Jones, Dempsey Dunkley-Clark, Sylvia Keogh, Helen Scott Lidgett, Stevie Stewart, Alan Jones, June Carroll, Wayne Hemingway, David Bristow and Jackie Jones. Thank you to photographer Roger Morton for his wonderful photographs from Dingwalls, (http://rogermortonphotographer.com), Harpreet Chohan at BOY London for permission to use images from the 1980 catalogue, photographer Peter Wood for images of Danny Lane and his work, Anna Smith for image advice, and David Fathers, (www.joemoon.co.uk), for his beautiful map of the Lock.

The cover image shows Siobhan Julia O'Dwyer and Carlos Gomez; many thanks to Jane MacDiarmid for her assistance.

I'm also indebted to Jack Whitehead, who gave up his time to share his extensive knowledge of Camden Town, Martin Sach at the London Canal Museum for historical advice and use of images (the memories of David Perman come from one of the many wonderful recordings at the museum, (http://www.canalmuseum.org.uk/), Sue Grimsdell for her enthusiasm and providing images from John Millar, (www.johnnymillar.com), and

Taking a breather on the pavement
outside the Lock

Jarek Klocinski, Rob Inglis, author of 'Canal the Musical', for permission to quote, Florence Salberter, Heritage Advisor at the former British Waterways, the staff at the Camden Local Studies and Archives Centre, Tess Hines at the Mary Evans Picture Library, Clare Hindson and Laura Wagg at the Press Association, Toby Mott for use of the Clash poster from The Mott Collection, and Michelle Featherstone for permission to quote from her song 'Camden Town', (www.michellefeatherstone.com/home.html). A final thanks to designer Arianna Osti and the team at Frances Lincoln.

Sources & Further Reading

Camden Locksmiths, Richard Carr, *The Guardian,* July 19, 1973
Camden Town 1791-1991 A Pictorial Record, Valerie Hart, Richard Knight and Lesley Marshall, London Borough of
    Camden Leisure Services Department, 1991
In Camden Town, David Thomson, Penguin Books, 1983
Camden Town, London's Weekly Street Festival, Michael Harrold, *The London Monthly,* May 1998
Camden's treasure box, Nicholas Tomalin*, Sunday Times,* July 1, 1973
Canal Arts and Crafts, Avril Lansdell, Shire Publications, 2004
Discovering Craft of the Inland Waterways, D.J. Smith, Shire Publications, 1977
Discovering London's Canal, Derek Pratt, Shire Publications, 1977
Enjoying a summer boat trip at London's craft community, Jean Scroggie, *Daily Telegraph*, June 26 1976
Exploring the Regent's Canal, Michael Essex-Lopresti, Brewin Books, 1987
Fight back against the clone invasion, Ruth Potts, June 17 2005, *Camden New Journal*
It's going to be fun, down at Camden Lock! Anne Sharpley, *Evening Standard,* April 13, 1973
The Growth of Camden Town: AD 1800-2000, Jack Whitehead, Biddles Limited, 1999
The jigsaw of Camden Lock, Simon Regan, *Scallywag*, March 1992 issue No 5
London's Canal An illustrated history of the Regent's Canal, Herbert Spencer, Putnam & Co Ltd, 1976
London Street Markets, Kevin Perlmutter, Wildwood House, 1983
The Markets of London, Alec Forshaw and Theo Bergstrom, Penguin Books, 1983
Mayhew's London, Henry Mayhew, edited by Peter Quennell, Bracken Books, 1984
Purple Passions, Narelle Muller, *Daily Express* April 30, 1994
Regent's Canal: A policy for its future, A Study by the Regent's Canal Group, 1967
Streets of Camden Town, Camden History Society, 2003
A Tale of Two Markets: For Seekers of Eclectic, Lisa Anderson, *Chicago Tribune*, 1987
Those Tourists are Money: The Rock 'N' Roll Guide to Camden, Ann Scanlon, 1997, Tristia
Through London By Canal 1885, a British Waterways Board Publication
Wartime St Pancras: A London borough defends itself, Charles Allen Newbery, Camden History Society 2006
Why Camden people aren't mourning the ruined market, Michael Hann, February 12, 2008, *The Guardian*

Useful websites

http://www.camdenlockmarket.com/
Camden Railway Heritage Trust http://www.crht1837.org/
http://www.canalmuseum.org.uk/
http://www.camdentownunlimited.com/
http://canalrivertrust.org.uk/
http://www.whenlondonbecame.org.uk/
http://www.friendsofregentscanal.org/

Visitors enter the Lock from the canal
towpath. Before the market opened,
the path was closed to the public

Credits

The publishers would like to thank those listed below for permission to reproduce the artworks and for supplying photographs. Every care has been taken to trace copyright holders. Any copyright holders we have been unable to reach are invited to contact the publishers so that a full acknowledgement may be given in subsequent editions.

pages 1,149 (bottom right), 153, 154-5 (far left and far right) John Millar; page 14 © Rob Inglis 'Canal' The Musical; pages 16, 18, 21, 22 (bottom), 25 (top right and left), 28, 29, 31, 32, 33 (top right), 34 (left and middle), 36 (bottom), 39, 40, 42 (top), 44, 45, 46, 47, 48, 59 (top right), 68, 74, 75, 76, 77, 79, 80 (top left and bottom), 83, 111 (bottom), 115, 117, 118, 120, 121 (top), 160 (top right), 175, back cover image, Northside Archives; pages 19 (top) © Mary Evans Picture Library, 26 (right) © John Gay/ English Heritage. NMR/Mary Evans Picture Library, 113 © Mary Evans Picture Library/Shirley Baker; pages 20, 22 (top) London Canal Museum; page 26 (left) © English Heritage Archive, John Gay; pages 30, 60-1, 63, 66, 67, 69, 81, 86-7, 114, 119, 124, Eric Reynolds Archive; pages 33 (bottom left), 70 (left), 71 (top right) Peter Wheeler; illustrations pages 37, 71 © Wilf Scott; page 38 Jackie Jones; pages 46 (bottom right), 49, 70 (right), 71 (left), 84 (bottom) Tony Mackintosh Archive; page 50 (top) The Mott Collection; page 50-1 Roger Morton; pages 53, 54, 55 (top), 72-3 Sarah Jones; page 55 (bottom) Sylvia Keogh; pages 56-7 Helen Scott Lidgett; pages 58, 59 (top left), 64, 65, 89, 91, 92 June Carroll Archive; pages 80 (top and right), 138 David Bristow; pages 82, 84 (top), 129 (bottom) © Press Association; 85, 102, 129 top © Getty Images, page 90 Jacey Sallés; pages 94 (top left), 95 Maggie French/British Waterways, 141 Maggie French; page 96 Hanne Landin; page 97, Binh Doan; pages 99, 100, 101 Wayne Hemingway; page 103 BOY; pages 104, 121 (bottom), 125, 131 (top), 132, 133 (top and right), Dempsey Dunkley-Clark; pages 105, 106-7, 109, 110 (top), Stevie Stewart; page 108, Ian Morris; pages 116, 127, 130, 131 (bottom) Alan Jones; page 134 © Michelle Featherstone 'Camden Town', pages 139, 140 *Camden New Journal*; page 157 David Gilkinson; page 161 Jarek Klocinski; pages 168, 171 (top left) Peter Wood for Danny Lane.

Index